More Award-Winning Science Fair Projects

Julianne Blair Bochinski

Illustrated by Judy DiBiase

WILEY

John Wiley & Sons, Inc.

To my father and mother, Edmund and Elizabeth Bochinski.
Thank you for being an important part of my life.
I am grateful for all you have given me, especially your time.
I love you very much.

Published by John Wiley & Sons, Inc., Hoboken, New Jersey
Published simultaneously in Canada.

Design and production by Navta Associates, Inc.

The publisher and the author have made every reasonable effort to ensure that the experiments and activities in the book are safe when conducted as instructed but assume no responsibility for any damage caused or sustained while performing the experiments or activities in this book. Parents, guardians, and/or teachers should supervise young readers who undertake the experiments and activities in this book.

For general information about our other products and services, please contact our Customer Care Department within the United States at (800) 762-2974, outside the United States at (317) 572-3993 or fax (317) 572-4002.

Wiley also publishes its books in a variety of electronic formats. Some content that appears in print may not be available in electronic books. For more information about Wiley products, visit our web site at www.wiley.com.

Library of Congress Cataloging-in-Publication Data:

Bochinski, Julianne Blair, date.
  More award-winning science fair projects / Julianne Blair Bochinski ;
illustrated by Judy J. Bochinski-DiBiase.
     p. cm
Includes index.
Summary: Presents thirty-five award-winning science fair projects, a section on how to do
a science fair project, updates to science fair rules and science supply resources, as well
as new material on useful web sites.
  ISBN 0-471-27338-4 (cloth)—ISBN 0-471-27337-6 (paper)
  1. Science projects–Juvenile literature. 2. Science–Experiments–Juvenile literature.
3. Science–Exhibitions–Juvenile literature. [1. Science projects. 2. Science–Experiments.
3. Experiments.] I. Bochinski-DiBiase, Judy J.,
ill. II. Title.
  Q164. B63 2004
  507'.8—dc21

                    2003009477

Printed in the United States of America

10 9 8 7 6 5 4 3 2 1

CONTENTS

PART III   Appendixes   187

FOREWORD

I first met Julianne Bochinski when she was a freshman in my science class at Mary Immaculate Academy in the fall of 1981. Julianne, like her fellow students, knew that one of the major curricula requirements toward achieving a grade in my science class was to complete a science fair project. Through the years, my announcement of the science fair project assignment has usually been met with sighs of dismay as students realize that a science project is no small task. However, Julianne's enthusiam for the assignment, as well as the enthusiasm of her classmates, was remarkably strong from the outset. The energy and dedication that this class gave to the science fair was like none I had ever seen before. There was a feeling of excitement in the air, and I knew that something special was happening. Julianne's topic was "Alcohol as a Fuel: Recycling Wastes into Energy." Her project, along with four other projects from my science class, became winning science projects at the 1982 Connecticut Science Fair. It was a year to remember. These five students together received the state trophy for representing the most outstanding school in the state for 1982.

I will never forget the events of that year, which inspired many talented and creative students in following years and, perhaps, paved the way to Julianne's journey into the world of science. She continued to volunteer her time to the Connecticut Science Fair after graduating from high school and afforded young people the opportunities that she experienced when she was a science fair contestant.

It is a known fact that students who do science fair projects and are exposed to science fair participation tend to develop valuable skills such as analytical thinking and creative problem solving. These tools assist them in dealing with real life situations. Not everyone will become a scientist, but this exposure will broaden their horizons and lead them to other worthwhile pursuits.

This book is a great resource not only for students but more important for teachers and parents who encourage and guide young people throughout their formative years. Julianne's journey took her along many avenues from studying science to becoming an attorney and author, both of which are rooted in the scientific field. Perhaps one day an idea germinating from this book will take a budding young scientist on an incredible journey of a profound and amazing discovery that leads to a Nobel Prize.

God's blessings,

Sister Mary Christine Jachowdik, D.M.
Assistant Fair Director and Member of
Board of Directors for the Connecticut
Science Fair

ACKNOWLEDGMENTS

It was a pleasure to meet and work with the many talented and dedicated individuals over the past year who assisted me in many ways with the writing of this book. As with the first two editions of this book, I give my praise and gratitude to Sister Mary Christine, assistant fair director and member of the board of directors of the Connecticut Science Fair. Sister Christine has served as a dedicated mentor and adviser to many award-winning science fair participants for over twenty years. She graciously authored the foreword to this new edition and I cannot thank her enough for all she has given me throughout the years. She is a role model for many and truly a terrific person.

I would also like to thank Kate Bradford, senior editor of general interest books at John Wiley & Sons for recognizing the importance and role that science fair participation plays in the education of today's youth and for giving me the opportunity to produce this all-new comprehensive edition.

Additionally, I would like to thank Science Service, Inc., once again for providing me with the listings of the state, regional, and foreign science fairs and for graciously allowing me the opportunity to meet with, interview, and photograph the many talented and incredible students, fair directors, and judges participating at the 2002 Intel International Science and Engineering Fair in Louisville, Kentucky. It was a memorable and exciting week for sure. Also, many thanks to the dedicated students, fair directors, and judges at the many state and regional science fairs I had the pleasure of attending over the past year who have given me their time and words of wisdom.

A special thank-you goes to my dearest Ed Burke, who did not realize what he was getting himself into when he accompanied me one day to a local science fair close to home—it led to a whirlwind adventure (read: mission) involving many more science fairs, not so close to home. I thank him for the time, patience, and encouragement he gave me while I wrote this edition.

Finally, I wish to thank my sister, Judy DiBiase, for creating the drawings in the book. Working with you is always filled with fun and laughter. I am so glad we are sisters.

Student Consultants

I would also like to thank the gifted and talented group of young scientists with whom I had the pleasure to work over the past year in writing up their ideas and projects, which appear in this book. All of these students have won at the state or regional level. The names of these students and their projects are listed below:

- Jonathan Sellon: Does the Composition of Rosin Affect the Sound a Violin Produces?
- Elizabeth Zipperle: A Hare-Raising Experience: Do Mendel's Theories on Heredity Apply to Rabbits?
- Diana Samandarova: Heat of Reaction
- Kristen Su: A Study and Comparison of the Quantity and Potency of Antioxidents among Various Teas
- Joshua Hoffman: Is There a Correlation between Toilet Paper Texture/ Thickness and Low-Flow Toilet Bowl Clogging?
- Craig Kaufman: Which Vegetable Plant Has the Greatest Development of Calluses after Being Cloned?
- Domenic Bonanni: Phase I: Sighted Individuals; Sight through Sound II: Can Shape and Color Be Visualized through Sound? Phase II: Visually Impaired Individuals
- Gemma Kite: Evaluating Peak Load and Noise Pollution in Different Types of Asphalt
- Adam Moussa: Effects of Garlic and Vitamin C on High Blood Pressure in Human Subjects
- Kip Corwin: The Chladni Effect: Is There a Relationship between the Frequencies Produced and Patterns Created Using Bowed Plates of Various Metals?
- Paul X. Boland: Natural Attic Ventilation
- Chelsea N. Grigery (Intel International Science and Engineering Fair participant): Legal Tender or Criminal Evidence?
- Jake LeBlanc: Can Mosquitoes Be Safely and Effectively Eliminated through Identifying The Variables That Attract Them?
- Danielle Wojtaszek: Does Coating Metals Prevent Their Corrosion? A Study of the Effect of Corrosion on Metals in Different Environments
- Sarah M. Hart: Are Rodents Territorial?
- Theresa Morelli: Can Water Hardness Be Determined through Soap Bubbles?
- Luke Orenec: Can Pascal's Triangle Be Found in Various Graphs and Patterns in Various Situations?
- Ashley Booth: Do Aluminum Pots, Pans, and Foil Leach Aluminum to Acidic Foods Cooked in These Mediums?
- Kelly Noles: Does Killing Soil Microorganisms Result in Better Plant Growth?
- Ryan Sypniewski: Which Type of Fire Retardant Is Most Effective in Reducing the Flammability of an Evergreen Tree?

INTRODUCTION

Recently, it was brought to my attention that *USA Today* awards outstanding high school graduating students during the academic year with the prestigious honor of being selected as part of their "All-USA High School Academic Team." After learning that a local student had just received this honor I was curious to read his biography along with the biographies of the other students who received the award from the well-known newspaper. In glancing through the article, I was not surprised to see that the winning students were all honors students from a variety of schools—public, private, and parochial; they hailed from different territories across the United States, from New Hampshire to Hawaii; came from diverse ethnic backgrounds; and each had a unique talent and hobby as unique as one student's syndicated cartoon in a popular teen magazine to another student's out-of-school life as a professional opera singer. Each student was a different scholarly, creative, and talented version of the next, which given the prestige of the honor, did not surprise me. However, as unique and individual as each outstanding student was, almost all of them shared one thing in common. Much to my great surprise (and immense satisfaction) about 95 percent of the student biographies made mention to outstanding science fair project achievement in either the Intel Science and Engineering Fair, the Intel Science Talent Search, or the Siemens Westinghouse competition.

I then started to wonder what made these students so special and what set them apart from their fellow students. I wondered whether these incredible students were the recipients of some sort of genius phenomenon—whether the gene pool awards a small minority with incredible talent or whether these students were just plain lucky to have the best teachers. Unfortunately, this type of thinking often becomes philosophical and does not lead to any logical conclusion. However, the more I thought about these students the one thing I became certain of is that no matter how smart these students may be, how easy or natural it has been for them to master a musical instrument, write a school newspaper, or draw a cartoon, somewhere along the way they had to learn the methodology of creating, developing, and carrying out a science fair project. Even the best of the best had to learn the rules, methods, and protocols that come with completing and submitting a science fair project. Once I became certain in my belief of this principle, I then came to solve part of the puzzle. It then seemed very clear that the common element these students shared that set them apart from other students was simply the drive, determination, and willingness to persevere and succeed long after others have given up. These students are obviously on the extreme end of the bell curve for academic achievement and certainly so many other factors may have played an important role in getting them to where they have gotten, but the common theme that prevailed was their devotion to a scientific subject or discipline.

Bearing all that in mind, the All-USA High School Academic Team is not only an inspiration for hard work and determination and where it can take you, but also, they are an inspiration for science fair participation and the tremendous benefits that it can provide for every student. They show us that any student can succeed in his or her quest for science fair project success so long as they have the determination and willingness to do so. Each of the All-USA High School Academic Team members who completed an award-winning project had to start somewhere. Each of them had to learn how to do a science fair project for the first time, and each of them had to learn about a specific scientific discipline and how to conduct an experiment for the first time. These initial experiments then led them to greater science fair project achievements.

This book is a companion book to my original book, *The Complete Handbook of Science Fair Projects* and was written to help you get started on the path to science fair project success whether this is your first project or whether you are looking for tips, ideas, and inspiration for what it takes to succeed in science fair participation.

This companion book gives you all the timely and useful information you need (including website links to key resources where applicable) to guide you through each and every phase of creating, submitting, and presenting your science fair project. However, as the level of sophistication of science fair projects has increased over the past several years this book contains the detailed outlines of 35 award-winning science fair projects that are examples of what students are working on in the new millennium. As with the original book, these new outlines come from real students who have won real awards for their work. New in this book are the inclusion of what I feel are very pertinent hypothesis and background information for each of the project topics to give you a foundation for the subject matter behind each of these projects, which may give you inspiration to build a different project or a variation on a particular project that is presented.

As with the original book, I have to caution you that the project outlines appearing in this book are merely recipes that you are encouraged to sample and not duplicate in place of your own project. As such, just because these students have won awards for these projects does not mean that the outlines are guaranteed to work for you in accordance with the procedures given, nor are you guaranteed to win an award by following any of these outlines. To this end, the results of the projects have been purposely eliminated and substituted by questions for you to think about and to give you an example of how to observe, analyze, and draw conclusions for your own project. The projects are provided only to give you an idea of the methodology behind the scientific method (see Chapter 2) after which you should model your project or to spark an idea for a different science fair project. Since many first-time science fair participants reading this book have never had the opportunity to visit a science fair to see what a science project involves, the outlines are also a way to bring the science fair home to them. These outlines show a range of skill and technique, from those used in simple projects for young readers to those used in sophisticated projects that have competed at the Intel International Science and Engineering Fair for experienced readers. Once again, take a look at the projects for inspiration and guidance but do not copy a project for your own. You will rob yourself of a wonderful learning experience. Nobody wins if a project is copied straight out of a book.

I want to conclude by saying that while a great many books on the subject of science fair projects have been written to help students and their parents "survive the challenge" of completing a science fair project, the purpose of this book and its prior related editions have always been to present a clear and comprehensive format for completing a project in a way that will help students and their parents see the challenge as a wonderful opportunity for achievement. Everything you need to get started and move forward through each phase of your project is here in this new book. Science fairs of the new millennium are exciting, fun, and rewarding opportunities to take advantage of. I hope that the tips, examples, and references contained in these pages will open your mind to the endless possibilities that await you and that perhaps someday you too will make the All-USA High School Academic Team!

PART

I

A Complete Guide to Science Fair Projects

1

SCIENCE FAIRS AND SCIENCE FAIR PROJECTS

What Is a Science Fair Project?

A science fair project is different from any other type of project you work on at school. Why? Because it is an independent educational activity that encompasses a variety of skills, many of which you have to teach yourself as you go along. A science fair project gives you hands-on experience and knowledge in your own independent field of study involving science, math, or engineering. It is a challenging extracurricular assignment that allows you to use your own ideas or a topic that you develop with your science instructor to investigate a scientific problem or question that interests you. You will not only be learning about a specific field of science and perhaps acquiring a unique skill in this field, but getting to know what it would be like to work in this field as an adult.

For example, you will learn how to investigate, network, conduct interviews, follow rules and guidelines, use various tools and equipment, analyze data, draft an abstract, write a report, prepare a display, and speak in public. With work and dedication on your part, the experience you will gain and the skills you will achieve from this extraordinary activity will be well worth all the time you put into it. The reason is plain and simple: as you make progress and begin to see your project develop and come together, your self-esteem will soar, and the project that was initially such a challenge, will eventually become a grand personal achievement—unique only to you.

What Is a Science Fair?

Every spring, thousands of students in grades 5–12 prepare science fair projects for competitions held by school districts, counties, and states. These fairs are public exhibitions of the students' projects to recognize their work and to stimulate interest in science. Professionals from the scientific community often judge the science projects. Students who participate can earn valuable experience along with educational grants, scholarships, and other prizes. Additionally, many college recruiters give science fair project participation high marks in considering an application for college admission.

Every year, thousands of students enter state, regional, or foreign affiliate science fairs of the Intel International Science and Engineering Fair like this recent state fair in Massachusetts.

When you participate in a local science fair, you have a chance to move on to a higher level of competition in a state or regional science fair. Today, most regional and state science fairs are charter affiliated with the Intel International Science and Engineering Fair (ISEF), which is considered the World Series of science fairs. (See Appendix D for a complete listing of state, regional, and foreign science fairs currently affiliated with Intel ISEF.) The grand finale of all state and regional science fairs in the United States and in several other countries is the Intel International Science and Engineering Fair (Intel ISEF).

The Intel ISEF is sponsored by Intel Corporation and several other major companies and organizations and is administered by Science Service, Inc., a national, nonprofit group based in Washington, D.C. In addition to the Intel ISEF, Science Service administers the Discovery Channel Young Scientist Challenge (for middle school students) and the very prestigious Intel Science Talent Search (formerly called the Westinghouse Science Talent Search) for high school students. These events are considered to be the most prestigious competitions in precollege science. (For more information about the Discovery Channel Young Scientist Challenge or the Intel Science Talent Search and other notable science fair project competitions, see Appendix E.) Science Service also offers wonderful programs and publications, including the weekly publication *Science News*.

What Is the Intel International Science and Engineering Fair (Intel ISEF)?

According to Science Service, the nonprofit organization that has administered this event for over 50 years, the Intel ISEF is the only international science fair project competition for students in grades 9–12 in the world. The top high school students from each Intel ISEF–affiliated fair are invited to compete at this prestigious convention, which is held annually in a major city, usually in the United States. The fair welcomes about 1,200 contestants, on average, from nearly 40 different countries. To see if there is a state or regional Intel ISEF–affiliated science fair near you, see Appendix D.

The Intel ISEF is, in a word, incredible! You would be awed by the sheer magnitude of this event, which hosts the finest science fair projects in the world, displayed by exhibitors from every part of the globe, many of whom come dressed in their finest suits or school uniforms. These exhibitors are often accompanied by an entourage of mentors, teachers, and families eagerly snapping photos and waving flags at awards ceremonies. Along with the exhibitors, there is an impressive group of Intel ISEF associates and judges who make up a Who's Who list in various scientific fields.

It is a scene like no other, except perhaps the Olympic games, and this is not an exaggeration. The annual event is a weeklong affair complete with opening and closing ceremonies, formal parties, awards presentations, workshops, networking meetings, sight-seeing tours, and of course intense judging rounds. Exhibitors compete for over $2 million in college scholarships, tuition grants, internships, and ultimately (for the top grand prize winners) a chance to attend the Nobel Prize ceremonies in Stockholm, Sweden.

When you consider the opportunities the Intel ISEF presents—meeting students who will be tomorrow's scientific leaders, networking with the best minds in science, gaining exposure to the scientific community, and possibly winning awards (some of which could pay your entire college tuition for four years)—your science fair project is sure to take on a whole new meaning to you. I wish you great success on your project. Perhaps someday you too may be invited to attend the Intel ISEF as a contestant. It is the experience of a lifetime.

If you would like more information about the Intel ISEF, the Intel Science Talent Search, the Discovery Channel Young Scientist Challenge, or an affiliated fair in your area, please write to:

Science Service, Inc.
1719 N Street, N.W.
Washington, DC 20036
Phone: (202) 785-2255
Fax: (202) 785-1243
E-mail: sciedu@sciserv.org
Internet: www.sciserv.org

The Intel ISEF Guidelines

If you've read up to this point, you might be wondering if your local county, state, regional, or country science fair is affiliated with the Intel ISEF. Chances are that it is. Therefore, the focus of this book is on creating, developing, experimenting, and presenting a top-notch science fair project according to the Intel ISEF rules and guidelines. The following sections are organized according to the steps that you should take in preparing a science fair project for such a fair.

2
BEFORE YOU GET STARTED

Basic Issues to Consider before Starting Your Project

Because you may be doing a science fair project for the very first time, you need to learn the basic parts of a science fair project (namely, the **scientific method**).

The Scientific Method

A science project studies a scientific problem in order to answer a proposed question or develop a better technique or final product. Science projects primarily involve research and tests to arrive at a specific conclusion. The basic procedure involved in a science project is modeled on a process called the **scientific method.** This method consists of the following elements: problem/purpose, hypothesis, research/procedure, experiment, and analysis of results or conclusion. The following list defines each element of the scientific method and provides a basic example of how you would develop a topic through the scientific method.

The Scientific Method by Example

Problem/Purpose: The problem or question for which you are testing or seeking to solve.

Example: Does an interrupted sleeping pattern or disturbed circadian rhythm affect one's alertness?

Hypothesis: Your educated guess about the solution to the problem and the results you expect to achieve from your experiment.

Example: I believe that sleep influences one's alertness and that an interrupted sleeping pattern or disturbed circadian rhythm would negatively affect one's alertness.

(Continued)

Research/Procedure: The process by which you gather information. This may include consulting reference materials, the Internet, mentors or professionals in the scientific field you are studying, or other persons or organizations related to your subject who will help you understand your topic and help you formulate how you will test your hypothesis through an experiment. At this stage you should carefully plan how the experiment will be carried out through time frames, variables, and controls, and how the results will be observed and measured.

Example: You may start with the premise that two groups of people will be studied. Group I will be allowed to sleep 9 hours without interruption. Group II will be allowed to sleep 10 hours but will be awakened every 2 hours for 15 minutes to give group members a total of 9 hours of sleep. Following the periods of sleep, both groups will be tested for alertness to determine whether their performance is influenced by the conditions to which they were subjected prior to the test.

As you continue through this stage you will need to keep fine-tuning your proposed experimental plan.

Example: What materials or subjects will you use to conduct your experiment? Will you account for variables such as age, gender, daily routine, amount of food consumed during the day, daily exercise routines, and so on? Do you plan to measure alertness through a written test that measures cognitive performance? Or do you plan to measure alertness through a physical reflex test? Finally, how many trials of your experiment will you conduct and how will you collect and analyze your data?

Experiment: The process by which you carry out the procedure you outlined during the research/procedure stage to test your hypothesis.

Analysis and Conclusions: The solution to your proposed question and proof or rejection of your hypothesis.

Example: Based on the data from this test, interrupted sleepers perform less efficiently than noninterrupted ones on an alertness test.

You will want to explain how the results may have varied among different conditions, subjects, and trials, as well as the value of your research. You may be able to suggest ways to improve the problem or experiment for future study. Finally, you may conclude by explaining the practical results and usefulness of your study.

Example: The results of this experiment varied between subjects of different ages, genders, and lifestyles but overall provide a similar conclusion: an interrupted sleeping pattern or disturbed circadian rhythm does affect one's alertness, both mentally and physically, which can become a serious problem over time. A more detailed study could be conducted to further refine the results. This project has important implications for professionals with interrupted sleep patterns, such as emergency medical technicians, doctors, and firefighters, who perform critical work and are often subjected to interrupted sleeping patterns.

Going Solo or Teaming Up

Before we move ahead to finding a great topic and getting started with it, you will need to decide whether you are going to work on your project alone or as part of a team with a fellow student or students. Most projects produced for science fair competition are by individual entrants. A smaller percentage are by team entrants and there is a very good reason for that. Team projects require joint commitment, shared interest, and a balanced work ethic from both partners, along with great interpersonal skills that will last over a period of time. Finding two or three students who match all of these qualities is not easy. Team projects can be very rewarding, but they are not for everyone. There are pros and cons to working with another student and you need to examine them carefully and make sure you are teaming up for the right reasons before you decide to commit to a team project.

Positive Reasons to Team Up

Many a scientist and engineer will tell you that in the real world they often have to work together with their peers as part of a team on a research project because each member of the team contributes a valuable skill or area of expertise

These talented young ladies' joint efforts worked so well that they not only won a trip to the Intel ISEF, but they also earned top awards in their category. Evening gowns? You bet! Besides an intense round of project interviews, the Intel ISEF also features many other activities, including a lavish formal dinner party for its international contestants.

different from the others. The synergy of the unique qualities of each team member creates a successful research or engineering project. Similarly, if you and a fellow student have complementary skills that would be useful on a given topic, a team project might be a great thing for both of you. For example, if both you and a partner are interested in a topic that requires biochemistry laboratory skills in which you have some experience or skill, and it also requires meticulous data collection and mathematical analysis skills, which your friend is a whiz at, it would be a shame to not collaborate with this person as a prospective partner.

Reasons Not to Team Up

Keep in mind that you are going to be working with your partner for several months or more. While you may be on the same side of the fence today, you may be on opposite sides in a short period of time, especially if one of you is doing all the work. Be sure you are teaming up with someone you can trust to work hard and be devoted to the best outcome of the science fair project. Do not team up with someone for the sole reason that he or she is your best friend or because you would like to be friends with him or her. While it is absolutely essential to work with someone you like and get along with (remember, you're both going to be tied into this project for a long time), it can be burdensome and destructive in the long run if you and your friend have a disagreement and take it personally. Both of you need to set some ground rules before you embark on a project together. Make sure that you agree on your joint responsibilities and duties to the project ahead of time, and make a pact that you will not let your friendship get in the way of the project or the other way around!

Summary

1. In its basic form, a science fair project is made up of a series of steps or a formula called the scientific method. Almost all science fair projects fit within the framework of the scientific method.
2. The scientific method consists of the following steps: problem/purpose, hypothesis, research/procedure, experiment, and analysis of results or conclusion.
3. Most science fair projects are conducted by individual students. However, a science fair project can also be a team effort. Before you get started on your project, you will need to know whether you will be going solo or working as part of a team. Be sure to consider the pros and cons of going forward with a team project before signing up for one.

3

GETTING STARTED

Select a Topic

Once you understand the foundation of a science fair project and how it works, it is time to select a topic for your own science fair project.

Believe it or not, selecting a topic for a science fair project may be the toughest part of the process. Every year many students planning to do a science fair project begin an unorganized search of the public library or the Internet through volumes and volumes of scientific articles and the latest scientific news stories without knowing what they are looking for. After several useless attempts at finding a subject to work on, most students become overwhelmed and frustrated. The Internet and public library are good places to find a topic, but most students are not focused when they begin their search. Without knowing what it is that you are looking for, it is almost impossible for you to come up with something that is going to work as a topic. The key is to have some direction before you begin. This chapter will help you select a topic that is both interesting and meaningful to you by showing you how to approach the selection process in a focused way.

Primary Areas for Finding a Topic: Your Interests, Experiences, and Resources

The first step in the process of selecting a topic is simple but extremely important: pick an area of science in which you have some particular interest, experience, or resources available to you. You may wonder if this is really necessary, especially if your science fair project is a required part of your science class grade for the semester. You may think that any project topic will do as long as it helps you to make the grade. If you are thinking this way, please think again. Even if you did not choose to do a science fair project, picking a topic that you are interested in or know something about is really important! There are several reasons why. First, you are going to be with your project topic for quite possibly a few months or longer. If you don't pick the right topic, you will be bored stiff! Second, if you want to do a top-notch job, you will need to choose something that you can feel passionate about. It's guaranteed to be reflected in your work. Third, you are going to have to live the life of a dedicated researcher for a period of time. If you don't have any idea what kind of work the project entails, you won't get very far. "A Study of the Applications of Single Crystal Carbon Nanotubes" may sound like a winning topic, but if you know absolutely nothing about this subject, have no experience with this area of science, and do not have the materials or resources to help you with this topic (see "Find a Good Mentor" later in this chapter), it's probably not going to work for you. Do yourself a favor and look closely at your interests, experience, and resources before settling on a topic. And remember, there is nothing worse than being unhappy with your topic and feeling like you're stuck with it. Do not be afraid to get out of it and find another topic if you do happen to become bored or disinterested with your original idea.

Think about Your Interests

One suggestion to help you in approaching your topic is to make a list of general science categories that you really like. Then go through your list and classify each category into subcategories of interest. For example, if one of the categories you listed was *medicine and health,* some subcategories might include *nutrition, diet,* and perhaps *vitamin supplements.* Chances are good that you will find yourself more interested in one area of science than another. Such preferences usually indicate good possibilities for topics. If, for example, you chose *vitamin supplements* as your subject, you should then try to identify a particular aspect of this subject that you want to investigate. For example, do you want to study the effects of plant compounds known as *polyphenols* in inhibiting the damaging effects of free radicals, or do you want to see how they interact with certain over-the-counter drugs? If one of the categories you listed was *zoology,* some subcategories might include *wildlife, birds,* and *environmental conditions affecting their lives.* If you chose *environmental conditions affecting the life of birds,* you should determine whether you want to study something like the atmospheric conditions that influence their migration, or how atmospheric conditions affect their life span. These are just a few examples of how you would develop a topic from your selected subject area. For more lists of scientific categories and subcategories that can be broken down into topics, see Appendix A.

Remember, your best choice for a topic is a subject in which you have a particular interest. While it is helpful to have some knowledge of the topic before you choose it, this is not essential. Unless you pick a topic that is very challenging, if you are interested and resourceful, you will learn what you need to know.

Think about Your Experiences

Another way to select a topic is to examine your past experiences. Do you have any skills or experience in a particular area of science? For example, perhaps you dismantled your personal computer to troubleshoot a problem and noticed that the microprocessor was rather hot. Perhaps you wondered if the heat would be detrimental to the microprocessor or if there was some type of device or material inside your computer that protected the microprocessor from the heat. Your curiosity might have led you to read about *heat sinks,* which are designed to draw heat from microprocessors. As you read about heat sinks you might have wondered if the metal composition of a heat sink would affect its ability to draw the most heat. Such an experience makes an excellent example of how you would derive a topic from a past experience.

Another way to find a topic from past experiences is to recall any unusual experiences you have had. For example, perhaps you once felt that your eyesight sharpened whenever you ate a certain vegetable, or perhaps you discovered a rare type of moss growing on a tree stump in your backyard that repelled insects. You may have wondered whether the material that enabled your watch dial to glow in the dark also emitted radiation that was affecting your environment. Or, you might remember personal experiences that lead you to investigate or conduct research because the subject was near and dear to you. For example, perhaps your beloved pet cat developed *feline fatty liver disease,* an often fatal disease for cats that usually does not show any symptoms until it is too late to treat. Your difficult experience with your pet cat might have led you to research the subject to see how you could help your cat, and it may have provided you with the opportunity to work closely with your family veterinarian in the diagnosis and treatment of your cat. Personal experiences such as these are excellent sources for project ideas.

Tap into Your Resources

While thinking about your interests and past experiences, do not forget the personal resources you have at your disposal. They are excellent to consult for a topic and can become very instrumental to you as you progress through your science fair project. So think about people you know and how they might be able to assist you in finding your topic. In the example of the *feline fatty liver disease,* such an experience might have fostered a good relationship with the family veterinarian, an excellent personal resource to consult about developing a zoological science idea into a science fair project topic. In the example, the family veterinarian might be able to assist you in your study and testing of *feline fatty liver disease.* The great thing about personal resources is that they are all around you and their advice is free (hopefully). These individuals do not have to be scientists, engineers, or doctors in order for you to tap into their background and find a great topic. For example, start in your own home. What does your mom or dad do professionally? If your dad works in building and construction, he might be a great resource for a topic that would investigate something like the durability of concrete. As you talk more and more with him about this subject you may be able to develop a topic such as *the effects of spray-coated fiber reinforcement on the strength of concrete.* If your cousin is an accomplished violinist, he or she might be a great resource for a topic that would investigate *instrument sound quality, pitch,* and so on. As you talk to him about the subject, you might come up with a topic such as *the effects of rosin on the sound quality of a violin.* If your next-door neighbor works for your state's department of transportation, he might make an excellent resource for a topic that might investigate traffic patterns, traffic lights, and rush hour traffic, which could lead to a topic in this area. Personal resources, such as family, friends, and professional contacts, can help you to find a great topic.

Secondary Areas for Finding a Topic: Scientific Abstracts, the Internet, Traditional Periodicals, and Current and Local Topics of Interest

Research Scientific Abstracts

Another possible source for a good topic is scientific abstracts. Abstracts can be located in bound scientific journals that are usually available at your local college or university library. These specialized journals are used primarily by science professionals. Articles are generally grouped into two classes: research experimental reports and reviews of scientific literature. Monthly issues are published in accordance with a cumulative subject and author index that is published annually. But remember, if you look through scientific abstracts, be sure to examine them in a field of study that you are interested in.

Research the Internet and Electronic Periodicals

Since so many great Web sites come and go over a short period of time, it was not feasible to list all of the great science fair topic idea Web sites online at the time this book was written. However, the 10 Web sites and electronic scientific magazines listed on the following page have great content and have been online for a while, so we hope they will still be around by the time you read this. They offer terrific resources and ideas that you can use to generate a science fair topic.

Research Magazines and Other Traditional Periodicals

Another area to investigate if you have not already thought of a topic is the periodical literature in your field of interest. Go to your local library and look through the most recent magazines and newsletters in the field you have chosen. These are effective aids in finding and researching a topic because they are concise and up-to-date. Magazines such as *National Geographic* (www.nationalgeographic.com), *Discover Magazine* (www.discover.com), *Popular Science* (www.popsci.com/popsci), *Popular Mechanics* (www.popularmechanics.com), *Mother Earth News* (www.motherearthnews.com), *Scientific American* (www.scientificamerican.com), and *Prevention* (www.prevention.com) and most computer and technology magazines are the best traditional journals to consult while searching for an original topic.

Research Current Topics or Local Topics of Interest

Keep in mind, too, that a successful project tends to be one that works with a new technology, problem, issue of current interest, or a novel approach to an ongoing

Ten Helpful Web sites for Science Project Ideas

www.scienceproject.com/index.asp   One of the largest Web sites for science project ideas, information and support.

http://school.discovery.com/sciencefaircentral/index.html   The Discovery Channel's science fair resource guide. Contains information on completing a project and a guide for teachers.

www.sciencenews.org   A publication of Science Service that contains interesting and timely scientific articles.

www.sciencedaily.com   Contains links to the latest science research news from which science project ideas can be developed.

http://whyfiles.org   Contains a real-life approach to scientific news stories from which science project ideas can be developed.

www.isd77.k12.mn.us/resources/cf/welcome.html   Cyber Fair. Contains science projects and information for younger students.

www.exploratorium.org   Web site of the Exploratorium Museum. Contains project ideas and interesting content.

www.spartechsoftware.com/reeko   Reeko's Mad Scientist Lab. Contains science project ideas and other interesting science project information.

www.sci-journal org/index.php   Sci-Journal is an online publication for science students. The journal, based in England, gives students the chance to publish work they have done in their science class so that other science students can read about it.

http://www.madsci.org   MadSci Network. This group of scientists can provide answers to your science project questions. A lot of other interesting information as well.

problem. For example, back in the late 1970s and early 1980s, the main concern of many Americans was the energy crisis issue, so projects that involved energy themes fared well at that time. In the 1990s and even today, environmental issues remain popular. And now, in the new millennium, many students have been interested in projects with themes concerning all aspects of wireless communications, antibiotic-resistant bacteria, urban planning problems, and medicine and health issues. A good place to look up current issues or technologies is America Online. Just type in the key words "health," "science," or "computers" and you will retrieve many recent news articles in these subject areas that can be helpful in finding a topic that is related to a subject of popular current interest. Also, while browsing America Online be sure to check out the key word "science fair." It brings up some helpful content and advice for doing a science fair project and includes a few message boards where you can interact with other students to get ideas or advice for your science fair project.

Often, a successful science fair project works with a technology or issue of popular current interest, or a novel approach to an ongoing problem.

Another area to tap into is your own backyard. Certain topics and problems are ideal for your geographic location. For example, a review of science fair projects at a current regional science fair in Texas revealed that some projects focused on issues relating to oil refineries, weather, and space science, while at a recent Florida regional fair, projects dealt with the eradication of insects, marine and aquatic sciences, and agriculture. These geographically localized areas of science can provide some terrific topics that may be ideal for you in terms of your location, whereas they might not be as ideal for students located elsewhere. Take advantage of where you live and your local resources.

Other Areas for Finding a Topic: Local, State, or Regional Science Fairs, and Science Fair Workshops

One of the best ways to get ideas is to surround yourself with them. If you are still having trouble finding a science fair project topic, try visiting a local school, regional, or state science fair. If you cannot get to the science fair in person, turn to Appendix B in the back of this book, which contains a list of over one hundred actual science fair project titles taken from award-winning science fair projects at a variety of recent state and regional Intel ISEF–affiliated science fairs. The topics are broken down by Intel ISEF categories of science. Or log on to the

This exhibitor at the Delaware Valley Science Fair literally found his science fair project in his backyard!

Internet and visit some of the Intel ISEF–affiliated science fair Web sites that are listed in Appendix D. You will get to see the quality of science fair project work performed by middle school and high school students at some of these Web sites, as well as what topics are current and interesting to you.

Attend a Science Fair Workshop

Many state and regional science fairs hold workshops for students during the summer and fall to help students understand the science fair project process overall, as well to show them how to focus in on a particular scientific field and

A word of caution: While it is beneficial to visit a local, state, or regional science fair to see what a winning science fair project looks like and to get ideas, do not attend a science fair for the purpose of copying another student's work. Not only would this be plagiarism, but you would not achieve success by showing up at the following year's science fair with the identical project that won at a previous year's fair. Science fair administrators and judges will easily remember a winning entry from a previous fair and would possibly disqualify your entry if they sense you copied another student's work.

narrow it down into a specific scientific question or problem for the upcoming year's science fair. Many of these workshops offer smaller sessions in various fields of science, mathematics, and engineering. By attending one of these workshops, not only will you be able to develop your science fair project topic, but, you will have the opportunity to meet some valuable contacts. You could even find a mentor to guide you in your research, and perhaps assist you in accessing valuable testing equipment or the facilities of a research laboratory. More information about working with a mentor appears later in this chapter.

Organize Your Investigation

Once you have found an area of science or a subject that satisfies you, you are ready to get started. At this time, it is necessary to organize yourself and take inventory. You can begin by getting a notebook to create a journal of everything you will be learning and doing for your project. A journal is the best way to organize your research, and what's more, it will serve as an excellent outline for your report. In your journal describe articles you have read, places you have visited, data results, and other points you think are worth noting. Write down important information so that you will not have to search through your references again.

Next, take into consideration the amount of time you have to complete the project, so that you can plan accordingly. As a researcher, you are investigating a particular problem or question. It would be helpful to know exactly what you are aiming for and how far you are willing to go to pursue your immediate objective. In addition to time constraints, you will need to take note of rules and guidelines established by your regional or state science fair, the contacts you will need to make, the resources and mentors you are going to need, supplies and equipment you will require, and finally the expenses you will incur.

Budget Your Time and Projected Expenses

Realize what you are getting into. Most science fairs are held from late February through late April. If you have been assigned to a science fair project by your teacher, you probably will know about the assignment as early as the preceding fall semester. That means you will have four or five months to do your project. However, keep in mind that due to the Scientific Rule Committee (SRC) guidelines that almost all state and regional science fairs follow, you will need to have your project proposal and description forms filled out and ready for submission as early as the November or December prior to the science fair in order to get approval for the work you are planning to do. If this is the case, then you will need to have your project topic and plan for experimentation worked out well before the SRC deadline. When selecting a topic, be sure that you can reasonably make the contacts you need, perform your research, obtain the necessary materials and carry out your experimentation, and analyze your results within the amount of time you have. (See Chapter 4, "Define Your Objective," for more information on streamlining your topic into a feasible experiment.)

You should also look at the expenses that may arise for the type of project you have selected. You may be able to borrow various supplies, materials, and equipment from your school, or you may be eligible to work at a university or laboratory that will donate their equipment and supplies; however, there are some supplies that you may have to purchase. Consult with your parents, teacher, or mentor first to see how much can be budgeted for your project and if it is affordable prior to settling on your topic. For a list of scientific supply companies that can provide an estimate of costs for some of the supplies you may have to purchase, see Appendix C in the back of this book.

Project Limitations and Required Forms

First and foremost, rules established by the Intel ISEF will govern your research on your topic and experimentation. The Intel ISEF's Scientific Review Committee (SRC) continuously reviews and updates its rules out of concern for the safety and protection of student researchers and their advisers, as well as to comply with local and federal regulations governing research. Some of the areas in which strict rules apply involve vertebrate and nonvertebrate animals; human subjects; recombinant DNA; human and animal tissues; pathogenic agents, including bacteria, fungi, and molds; controlled substances and chemicals; mutagenic agents;

A Scientific Review Committee (SRC) establishes strict rules governing the handling of certain subject matter, such as in this project that studied fungus growth on amphibians linked to increased UV B radiation.

carcinogenic agents; infectious agents; and hazardous materials or devices. For projects involving those areas, you are required to complete additional forms for the prescreening of your project and approval by an Institutional Review Board authorized by your state or regional science fair prior to the start of your research. You should contact your state or regional fair director for a copy of your fair's specific rulebook and forms. (See Chapter 4 in this book for more information about getting your project approved. And see Appendix D in the back of this book for a list of science fairs across the United States and worldwide that are charter affiliates of the Intel ISEF. A copy of the Intel ISEF rule book can be obtained from Science Service, Inc., at the address listed in Chapter 1 of this book.)

Make Connections and Contacts

A good way to begin work on your topic is to check all relevant periodicals and scientific abstracts at your local library and on the Internet. Look for the names, addresses, phone numbers, and e-mail addresses of resources with whom you can get in touch before you begin to work on your project. The contact information you find may also supply cross-references and referrals to key people and places, such as scientists, engineers, technicians, universities, organizations, laboratories, and businesses. Take advantage of these helpful references because they are your best source for learning what you may need to do, where to go, and who to meet before you do anything else.

As soon as you think you have located some useful physical or e-mail addresses, write a letter to the sources you have found. State that you are a student working under a deadline, discuss the plans you have in mind for your project, and describe the information you will need to gather. Ask for all the available literature that your referral might be able to recommend on your topic, along with any suggestions or advice for your experimentation. Ask for additional references of people in your area who are working in this field and who might be able to serve as mentors or offer you a connection to an institution. Ask your referrals if they know of an institution that might be able to assist you by donating their facilities or equipment to help you carry out your research or experiment.

Make several copies of this letter and send them to the people, organizations, and businesses who may be able to help you. Many will be glad to help, especially if your topic relates to their own products, technologies, or ideas. Not only does it benefit then by fostering good public relations, but also, it may help to get their business name and products out in the public eye. Sending out such letters enables you to save time by eliminating useless searches and honing your information down to the details that you need. Remember, you can always refer to textbooks, periodicals, and scientific abstracts when you need additional information later on.

Included on the following pages are two letters. One was sent by a student requesting information on alcohol as an alternative energy resource. This letter resulted in four informational guides that helped the student through her entire project. Along with the guides, she received lists containing the titles of exclusive literature on her subject and the address of an alcohol fuel producer who lived in her own county who served as a good mentor. The other letter was sent out by another student requesting information on x-raying corked baseball bats. This letter also helped the student make contact with a helpful mentor, which is perhaps the best way to get started on your project. The last section of this chapter discusses the benefits of working with a mentor.

Find a Good Mentor

One of the best-kept secrets of students who have had a very successful science fair project experience is their affiliation with a mentor. These students have had the opportunity to work under the advice and guidance of a professional scientist or engineer. A mentor can help you in many ways in the planning of your project, including helping you obtain materials and supplies, and possibly by enabling you to carry out your experimentation at a university, private corporation, or other testing facility. Students with a mentor often have a significant advantage over other students. This is especially the case at the high school level. If your goal is to make it to the top science fair competition in your state or to the Intel International Science and Engineering Fair, you really should consider making contact with a mentor.

Renewable Energy Information
P.O. Box 8900
Silver Spring, MD 20907

Dear Director:

I am a high school student currently working on a science project for my state's science fair. My project concerns the recycling of fermented organic garbage into ethyl alcohol. My objective is to see if it is possible for a household to construct a simple and inexpensive still capable of producing enough alcohol fuel to meet the household's energy needs. I also plan to compare ethyl alcohol with other natural fuel sources to determine its efficiency.

Recently, I found your address in an alcohol fuel directory. This guide mentioned that your organization would be able to assist ethyl alcohol fuel producers by providing them with suggestions and further information.

At this time, I would be grateful for any current information on alcohol production, still designs, and alcohol producers in my area. If possible, please send this information to me soon since I am working toward a February deadline.

If all goes well, this will be both an informative and stimulating project for me and my community.

Sincerely,

Student

Hillerich & Bradsby Company
P.O. Box 35700
Louisville, KY 40232-5700

Dear Sir:

I am an eighth grade student working on a science fair project that may be of interest to your company.

My project topic is "The Physics of Cheating in Baseball." Four bats were used to test my hypothesis which was that a baseball bat filled with sawdust, as opposed to a regular bat or bats filled with cork or rubber balls, will cause a baseball to travel the farthest on impact. I drilled out the center of three bats and filled one with sawdust, the second with rolled cork and the third with rubber balls. I left one bat alone to serve as a control. I tested the bats by placing each of them in a swinging device, which would hit a baseball placed on a batting tee when released. Out of the four bats, the sawdust-filled bat sent the baseball farther than the other bats.

In preparation for the State Science Fair, I would like to expand my project by seeing if it is possible to x-ray a baseball bat. I spoke with my doctor to find out if he or someone else would be willing to perform the X rays. He told me that I would have to find out whether a diagnostic machine X ray or metal fatigue/ stress fracture X ray would have to be performed. Please tell me which of these X rays would work with baseball bats.

Also, in doing my research I read an article, "The Physics of Foul Play" in *Discover,* in which tests were conducted at the request of MLB's Commissioner of Baseball. Do you have any information on how the bats were tested and what the results were? I would be grateful to have this information as soon as possible since I am working under a limited time frame. Thank you for your assistance.

Sincerely,

Student

Like all best-kept secrets and insider tips, a mentor is not easy to come by. To find a good mentor who works in the specific niche area of science to which your project pertains requires some effort, a little finesse, and a bit of luck on your part. Basically, the process involves networking, and that means you have to get out there and make connections through teachers, family, friends, and others before you will find that one person who will be a great resource to you and be willing to volunteer his or her time to work with you in the role of a mentor.

One way to make a connection with a mentor (if you do not have one through your school or family) would be to contact your local, state, or regional science fair. Many of these fairs have outreach programs for students that feature the volunteer support of professionals from the scientific community. Some science fairs have a very sophisticated program where you may have to file an application to qualify for a mentor since they usually have limited numbers of such individuals available. Additionally, a local university science department might be able to supply the name of a professor or graduate student who can help you. In any case, it is a good idea to try to seek out a mentor as soon as possible so that you will have enough time to discuss your project with that person, plan out the course of your research and experimentation, and get any necessary approvals.

Summary

1. Project topics can be found in a variety of different areas. Primary areas for finding a topic include focusing on your interests, experiences, and personal resources. Secondary areas for finding a topic include the Internet, traditional periodicals, scientific abstracts, and current and local topics of interest. Topics may also be found through visiting a local science fair or attending a science fair workshop.

2. Once you have found a topic that interests you, it is important to stop and analyze the feasibility of what you have chosen. Consider your time constraints, the rules and guidelines established by your regional or state science fair, the contacts you will need to make, the resources and mentors you are going to need, and finally, the expenses you will incur. Get a notebook to use as a journal in which you will record all your work.

3. Check all relevant periodicals and scientific abstracts at your local library and on the Internet for the names, addresses, phone numbers, and e-mail addresses of resources with whom you can get in touch before you begin to work on your project. Make contact with resources you have found in your research through writing letters or e-mails, making phone calls, and all other forms of networking.

4. Find a good mentor. Students with a mentor often have a significant advantage over other students. Finding a mentor requires networking with friends, family and others, so start looking early on in the process.

4

PLANNING AND CONDUCTING YOUR EXPERIMENT

The experiment can either make or break your science project. This is the backbone of the project, and you must put sufficient thought and preparation into it. You should plan to spend most of your time on a feasible experiment after researching. Your research should involve a practical application that includes measurements, analyses, or tests to answer a specific question. Judges look for these individual qualities and will be distracted if your project contains irrelevant facts and data.

Above all, make sure that the work you do follows the scientific method (see Chapter 2). Judges often see projects that are researched thoroughly and presented in a neat, attractive manner, only to find that they merely present a well-known idea, model, collection, or display that the public has seen too many times. Such exhibits are not experiments but mere demonstrations that do not merit high marks as science fair projects at the state and regional level. *Note however, that when working on an* **engineering project,** *you may in fact be constructing, designing, building, troubleshooting, or demonstrating a working model of a new product, a device to improve on an existing model or product, or an inventive model or device that addresses or solves an existing problem.* This is the nature of an engineering project and the judges expect it. However, even at the core of an engineering project there is a question or problem that is asked and addressed by the model, design, or device built.

In general, while preparing your project, try to present a question or problem and then prepare a series of tests to solve the problem or support a proposed hypothesis. If you follow the scientific method, your project should be easier to complete and will provide more meaningful results than if you do not use this method.

Because you want your results to be absolutely accurate, you should record all your data in your journal, regardless of whether or not they support your hypothesis. Your project will not be scored low or disqualified simply because your results did not support your hypothesis. You may develop your project by interpreting your end results and explaining why they were different from what you expected.

Keep in mind that judges do not expect you to come up with a revolutionary idea. They are more interested in seeing how much ingenuity and originality you

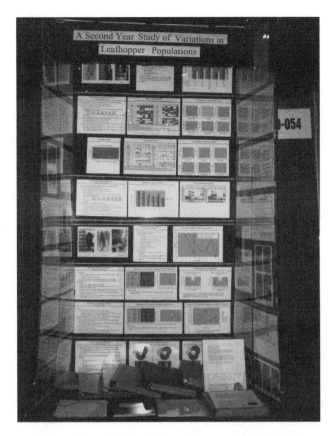

Some contestants continue to work on the same project for a second year's science fair because their original project experiment yielded results that opened new avenues of exploration for a second project study.

applied to an existing problem you are studying and the approach you took toward your problem. Most projects have been done before in one form or another. They usually differ to the extent that they are different approaches or applied techniques of an original idea or a confirmation of a conclusion under varying circumstances. Some contestants even submit the same project the following year at the same science fair because they have made significant progress in their topic since their first entry. Judges are mainly interested to see whether you chose the best method possible in your investigation, whether you have made the most effective use of materials, equipment, and techniques pertaining to your topic, and whether you have recorded and analyzed your data accurately and effectively.

Step One: Define Your Objective

Before you begin, streamline your proposed question. Decide what you want to prove, and try to attack the most important aspect of your topic. For example, if you chose oil spills as your topic, you would probably research its hazardous byproducts, cleanup solutions, and long-term effects on the environment. Such a broad topic would yield a variety of details without a specific focus or purpose. You must confine your topic to a single purpose or question. You can do this by listing all the different approaches that may be taken in your project through experimentation. Some of these might include:

1. Determining the effects that oil spills have on the growth of organisms.

2. Comparing health and disease statistics between different oil spill sites.

3. Determining the efficiency of a proposed solution such as bioremediation to neutralize and clean up oil from a spill.

After you have listed various approaches to your project, choose one that you think will produce a reasonable and practical experiment.

Given these choices, the first and second alternatives would probably be too broad to work with. Such experiments would require several years for you to compare the growth, health, and disease characteristics of several sites. The work would involve periodic studies of people, animals, and plants, in order to measure their overall health, function, endurance, immunity, and quality of vital functions. Although these are very challenging objectives that would make great long-term studies, they might be too much to satisfy your immediate objective within the time frame you have. However, the third alternative would be a great experiment because it focuses on a central idea, namely, it would study the efficiency of bioremediation (a natural means of using various microorganisms to consume fuel-derived toxins and turn them into carbon dioxide). You could measure the efficiency of various microorganisms in order to find out which one best eliminates oil in seawater. A procedural plan could easily be developed to parallel your purpose.

Step Two: Obtain Scientific Review Committee (SRC) Approval

Since many local, state, and regional science fairs are affiliated with the Intel ISEF, the format and instructions in this book are designed to help you create and present a science fair project that complies with Intel ISEF rules and guidelines. As such, it is important to provide a summary of Intel ISEF science project research and experimental guidelines that may affect your project. As soon as you have narrowed in on a project topic and defined your objective, you should consult with your science teacher or mentor about receiving Scientific Review Committee (SRC) approval before starting your project. Many local, state, and regional science fairs establish SRC approval deadlines long before the deadline for even entering your project in a science fair. Often this deadline is in November or December prior to the date of the science fair. The purpose of the SRC is to ensure the safety of the student performing the research and experiment as well as the subject being tested. The SRC also functions to disapprove research that may be inappropriate or illegal. Projects involving humans, vertebrate animals, pathogenic agents, or recombinant DNA must have SRC approval prior to the start of research.

Your science teacher or mentor is likely to be familiar with the rules and guidelines concerning SRC approval and probably has all the forms and paperwork you need in order to be in compliance. If not, contact your local, state, or

Research Plan (1A)

This completed form is required for ALL projects.
Type or print all information requested.
Answer all questions and complete Research Plan Attachment (see page 36)

1) Student's Name _____ Grade _____

2) Title of Project _____

3) Adult Sponsor _____

4) Is this a continuation from a previous year? ☐ Yes ☐ No
   If Yes: a) Attach previous year's **abstract & completed 1A & research plan** and
   b) Explain how this project is new and different from last year on **Continuation Form (7)**

5) This year's laboratory experiment/data collection began: _____ and ended: _____
   (must be stated)   (month/day/year)   (mo

6) Where will you conduct your lab work? (check all that apply) ☐ Research Institution ☐ School ☐

7) Name, address & phone of school and work site(s):
   School: Work site: Work site:

8) All projects require completed forms: Checklist for Adult Sponsor/Safety Assessment Form
   Research Plan (1A), Research Plan Attachment and Approval Form (1B) and may require
   Research Institutional/Industrial Setting Form (1C).
   Check ALL items that apply to your research.
   The following areas require review and approval by SRC or IRB prior to experimentation :

   ☐ **Humans** (requires prior IRB approval; complete Forms: Checklist, 1A, 4A [1C, 2, 5, 4B, if required])
   ☐ **Non-Human Vertebrate Animals** (requires prior SRC approval, complete Forms: Checklist, 1A, 1B, 2, 5 [1C, 3,
   ☐ **Recombinant DNA** (requires prior SRC approval, complete Forms: Checklist, 1A, 1B [2, 5, 1C, as required])
   ☐ **Pathogens** (requires prior SRC approval; complete Forms: Checklist, 1A, 1B, 2 [1C, 3, if required])
   ☐ **Controlled Substances** (requires prior SRC approval: complete Forms: Checklist, 1A, 2 [1C, 3, if required])
   ☐ **Human/Anim**

   ☐ **Hazardous**

9) Complete Resea

10) An abstract is r

International Rules for

Checklist for Adult Sponsor / Safety Assessment Form (1)

This completed form is required for ALL projects and
must be completed prior to experimentation

Student's Name _____

1) ☐ I have reviewed the **Research Plan (1A)**, Research Plan Attachment and signed Approval Form (1B).

2) ☐ The student and a parent / guardian have signed the **Approval Form (1B)**.

3) ☐ This project involves the following area(s) and requires **prior approval** before experimentation begins:

   ☐ **Human Subjects**   ☐ **Controlled Substances**
   ☐ **Non-Human Vertebrate Animals**   ☐ **Recombinant DNA**
   ☐ **Pathogenic Agents***   ☐ **Human or Non-Human Vertebrate Animal Tissue**
   * All bacteria, fungi, etc. isolated from the environment should be considered potentially pathogenic.

4) ☐ This project does not involve any of the research areas listed in #3.

5) ☐ This project involves human subjects. The student will obtain approval from an **Institutional Review Board (IRB)** before experimentation is started. (See pp. 12-13.)

6) ☐ This project involves non-human vertebrate animals, pathogenic agents, controlled substances, recombinant DNA, or human and animal tissue. The student will obtain approval from a **Scientific Review Committee (SRC)** before experimentation is started. (See pp. 15-24.)

7) ☐ This project involves the hazardous substances or devices checked below. A Designated Supervisor will provide proper supervision to the student. Prior approval by the adult sponsor and certification by a designated supervisor is required. (See p. 25.)

   ☐ **Chemicals** (i.e., hazardous, flammable, explosive or highly toxic; carcinogens; mutagens and all pesticides.) I have reviewed with the student the Material Safety Data Sheet (MSDS) listing for each chemical that will be used. I have also reviewed the proper safety standards for each chemical including toxicity data, proper handling techniques, and disposal methods. For *Safety in Academic Chemistry Laboratories*, write to the American Chemical Society, Career Publications, 1155 16th St., NW, Washington, DC 20036 (202/872-4512).

   ☐ **Equipment** (i.e., a sudden, heavy voltage greater than 220 volts). I have reviewed with the students the proper precautions for the equipment to be used by the student. For information about the Food and Drug Administration, Office of Compliance, 2098 Gaither Rd.,

   the student the proper safety standards for firearms use.

   ve reviewed the proper safety standards for each radioactive substance the

   nshielded ionizing radiation of 100-400 nm wavelength). I have reviewed with the concerning the type of radiation the student will use.

   Signature _____ Date of Review _____

   Research: Guidelines for Science and Engineering Fairs / 2001-2002   Page 34

Approval Form (1B)

This completed form is required for ALL projects.

1) **REQUIRED FOR ALL PROJECTS.**

   a) **Student Acknowledgment:** I understand the risks and possible dangers to me of the proposed **Research Plan (1A)**. I will adhere to all International Rules when conducting this research.

   Student's Printed Name _____ Signature _____ Date Acknowledged _____

   b) **Parent/Guardian Approval:** I have read and understand the risks and possible dangers involved in the **Research Plan (1A)** and Attachment. I consent to my child participating in this research.

   Parent/Guardian's Printed Name _____ Signature _____ Date of Approval _____

   c) **Adult Sponsor Approval:** I have read the Research Plan (1A) and Attachment prior to experimentation and reviewed the **Checklist for Adult Sponsor** with the student. I agree to sponsor the student named above and assume reasonable responsibility for compliance with all International ISEF Rules as they pertain to the **Research Plan (1A)**.

   Adult Sponsor's Printed Name _____ Signature _____ Date of Approval _____

2) **REQUIRED FOR PROJECTS REQUIRING SRC/IRB APPROVAL. SIGN 2a OR 2b AS APPROPRIATE.**

a) Required for projects that need prior SRC/ IRB approval BEFORE experimentation (i.e., see Item #8 on Form 1A.)		b) Required for research conducted at all Registered Research Institutions with no prior fair SRC approval.
The SRC/IRB has carefully studied this project's **Research Plan (1A)** and Attachment and all the required forms are included. My signature indicates approval of the Research Plan (1A) before the student begins experimentation.	**OR**	This project was conducted as a registered research institution (not home or high school) and was not previewed and approved by the fair SRC before experimentation, but it does comply with the International Rules. Attach (1C) and required institutional approvals (e.g. IACUC, IRB)

   SRC/IRB Chair's Printed Name _____   SRC/IRB Chair's Printed Name _____

   Signature _____ Date of Approval _____   Signature _____ Date of Approval _____
   Check one: ☐ Local or ☐ Affiliated Fair   Check one: ☐ Local or ☐ Affiliated Fair

   NOTE: If a stamp is used, it *must* be initialed by the chairperson.

3) **FINAL ISEF AFFILIATED FAIR SRC APPROVAL. (REQUIRED FOR ALL PROJECTS)**

   SRC Approval After Experimentation and Shortly Before Competition at Regional/State/National Fair
   I certify that this project adheres to the approved Research Plan (1A) and Attachment and complies with all International Rules.

   Regional SRC Chair's Printed Name _____ Signature _____ Date of Approval _____

   State/National SRC Chair's Printed Name _____ Signature _____ Date of Approval _____
   (where applicable)

   International Rules 2002/2003   full text of the rules and electronic copies of forms are available at www.sciserv.org/isef   Page 42

Here are a few sample forms taken from the Intel ISEF rule book. These forms are representative of forms that are required by science fairs throughout the United States and around the world that must be completed prior to commencing work on a science fair project that will be entered in a science fair competition.

regional science fair administrator to obtain SRC deadlines and the appropriate forms. For a complete listing of all current Intel ISEF–affiliated science fairs, please see Appendix D at the back of this book.

Step Three: Organize Your Experiment

Once you have reduced your topic to a single purpose or question, you must organize your experiment. In the example regarding bioremediation of oil spills, you must organize an experiment that will allow you to measure the efficiency of various microorganisms in neutralizing the presence of oil in seawater. It would be difficult (not to mention illegal) to add home heating oil to a body of water for the purpose of testing bioremediation over a short time period, so a more practical thing to do would be to collect several large buckets of natural seawater that you can add home heating oil to along with your microorganism variables and test in an environmentally safe area. Your objective would then be to study the effects of various microorganisms in the bioremediation of home heating oil. After you have organized your experiment, you must develop a procedural plan.

Step Four: Create an Experimental Procedural Plan

An experimental procedural plan is a uniform, systematic approach to testing your hypothesis. When you begin this phase you should make a step-by-step list of what you will do to test your hypothesis. To start, first *correlate* (i.e., bring one thing into a reciprocal relationship with another) what you want to prove. You begin by selecting one thing to change in each experiment. Things that are changed are called *variables*. You want to be able to correlate two or more variables—the *dependent* variable and the *independent* variable. The dependent variable is the one that is being measured; the independent variable is the one that is controlled or manipulated by the experiment. For example, you may want to see whether the health and growth of a tomato plant (the dependent variable) is influenced by the amount of light the plant is exposed to (the independent variable). The correlation here is between the health of a plant and light exposure. Several other independent variables may be used instead, such as water, oxygen, carbon dioxide, nitrogen levels, and so on. However, for the sake of clarity we will use only light as a variable for this example. You should then state how you will

This student posed the question, "Does an Asphalt Road or a Concrete Sidewalk Create Less Friction than a Linoleum Floor" for his project topic. Here, the correlation was between surface type and amount of friction.

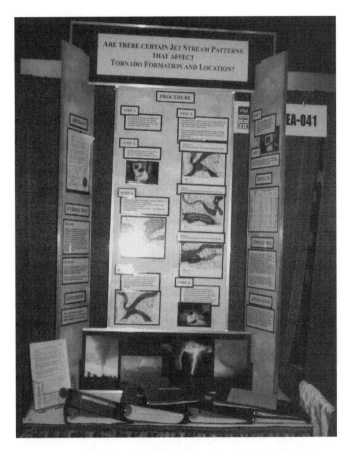

This project looked at the correlation between jet stream patterns and the formation and location of a tornado.

change your independent variable and how you will measure the amount of change in the dependent variable.

Establish a Control Group

Next, an experimental group and a control group must be established. The control group provides you with a basis for comparing the experimental group. For example, you may have an experimental group of tomato plants, which is placed in a sunny window for two weeks and watered periodically. At the end of the period, the plants have grown three inches and are very green. At this point, you may conclude that sunlight does indeed increase plant growth. But before you draw this conclusion, you should determine whether the tomato plants would have grown and become green without any sunlight at all. This is where a *control group* of plants is needed. A control group is used for purposes of comparison with the experimental group so that you can see what occurred by changing your variables.

The control group of plants in our example would be those plants that are given the same treatment as the experimental ones, with the exception that they would not be exposed to sunlight. If the outcome of the experiment were a significant difference between the two groups, then you probably would be justified in concluding that tomato plant growth is influenced by the amount of sunlight the plant receives.

The procedural plan in this example is very simple, but it gives you an idea of the process of an experiment. In essence, the procedural plan advances from one stage to another in an organized fashion. Remember, however, that most experiments are not as simple as the one described here. Often obstacles arise and other interesting characteristics of the subject are revealed in the process. You may even discover existing differences in several trials with only one variable. In fact, this is a frequent occurrence, and it is an important reason why you must keep accurate data records (see Chapter 5).

Step Five: Conduct Your Experiment

Once you have established your procedural plan for your experiment and have received approval, it is time to collect the materials you will need. You may also need to obtain approval or permission to work in a laboratory or other professional environment. The important thing to keep in mind as you put your procedural plan into action is to collect accurate data results from repeated trials with the same variables and record all of your data for later analysis (see Chapter 5 for this important next step). The benefit to taking this approach is that it increases the accuracy of your results and conclusions. How many times do you need to repeat your experimental procedural plan? This really depends on many different factors, not the least of which is your subject matter.

Note: Appendix C in the back of this book contains the listings of several science project supply companies that may be able to provide you with the supplies and equipment you need to carry out your experiment. However, if you have a mentor who is a professional scientist or engineer, you may already have the supplies and equipment you need through the mentor's affiliation with a university or company research laboratory.

Avoiding a Failed Experiment

There are several reasons why an experiment may fail to validate a hypothesis, prove a point, or simply do what it was intended to do, for example, mistakes in the way the experiment was carried out (procedural errors), a poor or incomplete final analysis, and an erroneous hypothesis.

Procedural Errors

To avoid procedural problems, you must be consistent and meticulous with your subject variables and controls over repeated trials. For example, in the experiment involving sunlight and tomato plants, if you gave the experimental group of tomato plants more water than the control group or planted them in a soil that contained more nitrogen, you would get artificial results. This means that you are failing to control or hold your variable constant. How can you determine whether it was the sunlight alone or in combination with other factors that made the experimental tomatoes flourish? The same problem with inconsistent maintenance of controls might apply if you were studying the behavior of your friends at a party for a psychological experiment. What would happen if you made your study obvious by taking notes or pictures? Your friends probably would be influenced by your behavior and would not act in their usual manner. In this case, as the old saying goes, "you cannot measure an experiment without affecting the result." These examples involve manipulated experiments that would yield useless data. Of course, other procedural problems may arise during an experiment, especially if poorly calibrated measuring instruments are used.

Poor Final Analysis

Even after a carefully controlled experiment is completed, errors can still occur, possibly resulting from an incorrect analysis of results. For example, if you concluded that a certain salve cures acne, on the basis of tests that were conducted on female adolescents but not male ones, your final analysis would be inconclusive. While the salve may have worked on the females you tested, it may not work on females in different age groups or on males of all age groups. Other problems with the final analysis may arise from mathematical errors or from data that are irrelevant to the topic.

Erroneous Hypothesis

When an experiment is completed, the results are sometimes quite different from those that were predicted. If this occurs, do not manipulate the results to fit the initial hypothesis. The hypothesis may have been incorrect or vague to begin with, and the experimental results were accurate. If such problems occur in your project, you can salvage your work by finding out why the results were different than expected or by explaining a new or unexpected observation or solution. This will show the judges that you understand the primary aspects that concern your project topic, including the control and handling of variables in experimentation, repeated trials, and approach to reaching conclusions. This actually happens to be a judging criterion that many students overlook. So, if your experimental results are different from what you expected after several trials, take advantage of this situation by thoroughly analyzing and knowing why you received the results you did. (For more information about the criteria judges look for when judging a science fair project, see Chapter 7.)

Keep in mind that many scientific investigations do not support their specific goals. However, this does not weaken the validity or value of these investigations. In fact, many experiments require repeated testing and exploration to understand a particular phenomenon. Sometimes, unexpected experimental results lead to surprising discoveries and more interesting science projects!

Summary

1. The experiment is an essential part of your science project. It should test, survey, compare, and ultimately aim to solve or answer the problem or question presented.

2. You must focus your topic on an experimental approach that will clearly test your hypothesis and will uphold the scientific method.

3. After you decide on an experimental approach, you must develop a way of testing your subject. This involves defining your objective, obtaining Scientific Review Committee approval, organizing your experiment, and creating an experimental procedural plan.

4. An experimental group containing variables and a control group must be established as part of the experimental procedural plan. Several trials should be made with the same variables to ensure consistent data results from which conclusions can be made.

5. Three common ways in which an experiment can fail are procedural errors, poor final analysis, and an erroneous hypothesis.

5

ORGANIZING AND PRESENTING DATA

A vital part of the scientific method is being able to analyze your results and observations (data) so that you can form a sound conclusion. This is basically performed through two means of analyses: qualitative analysis and quantitative analysis. Qualitative analysis is not based on measurements, rather it is a means of analysis that provides your observation; for example, "what components were found in a sample," or "whether an experimental group of plants performed better than the control group of plants." Quantitative analysis, on the other hand, is based purely on measurements and always involves numbers—for example, "how much of a given component is present in a sample," or "how much the experimental group of plants grew in comparison to the control group of plants." While qualitative analysis is important to the explanation of your results, it is quantitative analysis that truly expresses your ability as a student scientist to interpret your data in a more precise and objective way that will provide a useful means for the interpretation of your conclusions by others. The remainder of this chapter is devoted to the interpretation, use, and explanation of the numerical data you have gathered from your experiment.

A very important part of explaining your results and observations to others is by giving meaning to your numerical data and the conclusions you formed from it. Since you began your experiment, you have been gathering data. Data are essentially groups of figures for a given experiment. During the initial stages of an experiment, they may have little meaning so it is important that you compile and organize your data accurately for your final analysis, observations, and conclusions. A good way to keep data is to record them in your project journal. After you have written down all the experimental results in an organized way, you can easily refer to your results to make generalizations and conclusions. There are several methods of presenting data, including the basic tabular, graphic, and statistical methods.

Tabulating and Graphing

Raw data have little or no meaning in and of themselves. It is only when they are organized into tabular and graphic forms that they can be understood in terms of your project. The data results must be arranged so that a project observer or judge can quickly comprehend the results of the project at a glance. Tables are relatively simple to make and convey information with precision. Additionally, they form the basis for most graphs. The main points to consider are organization and coordination. For example, consider these recordings in tabular form of the body temperature of a flu patient:

Times	Body Temperature (°F)
6:00 A.M.	97.0
8:00 A.M.	98.0
10:00 A.M.	99.0
Noon	100.0
2:00 P.M.	101.0
4:00 P.M.	102.0
6:00 P.M.	103.0
8:00 P.M.	102.0
10:00 P.M.	100.0
Midnight	98.0

If you want to see how the patient's temperature fluctuated during the day, you can do this by analyzing the table. But if you wanted to see at a glance how the patient's temperature changed, a graphic representation would be more effective.

A line graph may be used for this analysis. A line graph is composed of two axes: the x, or horizontal, and the y, or vertical. The x axis contains all the points for one set of data, and the y axis contains all the points for the other set of data.

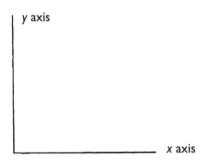

For example, you could label a range of body temperatures on the y axis and label the times on the x axis. After your axes are labeled, simply plot the points. Plotting involves matching each temperature with the corresponding time and marking them on the graph. For example, at 6:00 A.M. the body temperature was 97 degrees Fahrenheit, so you should locate and mark the point on the x and y axes at which 6:00 A.M. and 97 degrees correspond. Then do this for the rest of the data and connect the points to complete the graph.

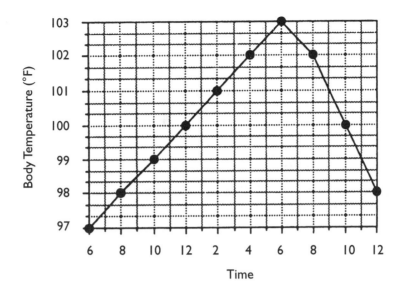

From this graph, we can quickly see that the patient's body temperature rose gradually, peaked late in the day, and fell during the evening.

Another means of graphical representation that makes data easy to understand is the pie chart. Suppose that you are testing a specimen of blood to determine the percentage of its composition of erythrocytes, leukocytes, and thrombocytes. After several tests and microscopical observation you conclude that the blood contained the percentages shown in the following table:

Cell Type	% Composition
Erythrocytes	50.0
Thrombocytes	38.0
Leukocytes	12.0
	$\Sigma^* = 100.00\%$

The data can be represented in a pie chart:

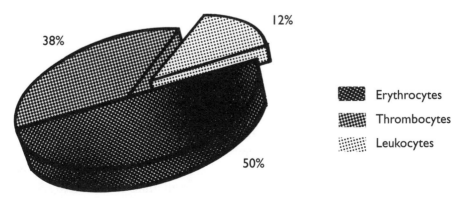

*Σ is a Greek symbol that means "the summation of."

Each section represents a percentage of the pie. It is easy to see that the leukocyte blood count is low in terms of its percentage of the total composition.

There are many other ways to graph your data besides the two methods shown. The important thing to remember about graphing is that it summarizes your results in a visual form that emphasizes the differences between groups of data results. As the old saying goes, a picture is worth a thousand words.

The Statistical Method

Some very simple statistics will allow you to expand on your data analysis. Some of these applications include: the *mean, frequency distribution,* and *percentile.*

The **mean,** expressed as $\bar{x}$, where x is any rational number, is a mathematical average that is really the central location of your data. The sum of your data numbers is denoted by the symbol Σ, which means "the summation of." This sum is then divided by the quantity of your data recordings, which is the symbol n. Thus the mean is expressed as this formula:

$$\bar{x} = \frac{\Sigma x}{n}$$

For example, consider the mean fluoride level in parts per million (ppm) from 11 different water departments.

Town Name	Fluoride Level (ppm)
A-Town	1.00
B-Town	1.50
C-Town	1.50
D-Town	0.05
E-Town	0.04
F-Town	1.01
G-Town	0.09
H-Town	0.05
I-Town	2.00
J-Town	1.00
K-Town	1.00
	$\Sigma(x) = 9.24$

Using the formula, you can express your results as follows: If $\Sigma(x) = 9.24$ and $n = 11$, then $\bar{x} = 9.24/11 = 0.8400$. The figure .8400 is the mean, or the mathematical average, of the studied water plants.

Now suppose that you collected samples from 50 water plants. It may be difficult to generalize about the results, so a better method is needed to record the data. One way of describing the results statistically is with a **frequency distribution.** This method is a summary of a set of observations showing the number of items in several categories. For example, suppose that the following levels were observed to be present in 50 samples:

Fluoride Levels (ppm)	Frequency (f)
2.0	3
1.70	6
1.50	7
1.00	8
0.90	10
0.80	7
0.50	6
0.04	3
	$\sum f = 50n$

These results can then be graphed using a histogram, which represents your frequency distribution. With a histogram, your item classes are placed along the horizontal axis and your frequencies along the vertical axis. Then rectangles are drawn with the item classes as the bases and frequencies as the sides. This type of diagram is useful because it clearly shows that the fluoride levels are normally at the 0.90 to 1.00 ppm mark (see diagram).

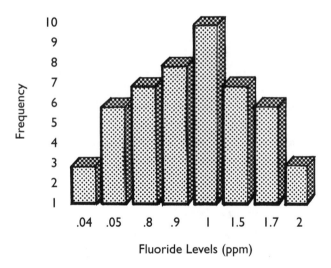

The **percentile** is another useful statistic. A percentile is the position of one value from a set of data that expresses the percentage of the other data that lie below this value. To calculate the position of a particular percentile, first put the values in ascending order. Then divide the percentile you want to find by 100 and multiply by the number of values in the data set. If the answer is not an integer (a positive or negative whole number), round up to the next position of the data value you're looking for. If the answer is an integer, average the data values of that position and the next higher one for the data value you're looking for. For example, suppose that you wanted to test the efficiency of 11 automobiles by measuring how many miles each car gets to a gallon of gasoline. You have recorded the following data: 17.6, 16.4, 18.6, 16.1, 16.3, 15.9, 18.9, 19.7, 19.1, 20.2, and 19.5. First, you would arrange the numbers in ascending order: 15.9, 16.1, 16.3, 16.4, 17.6, 18.6, 18.9, 19.1, 19.5, 19.7, and 20.2. Now suppose that you want to determine which car ranked in the 90th percentile. To calculate the 90th percentile for this data set, write this equation: $(90/100)(11) = 9.9$. Since 9.9 is not an integer, round up to 10, and the tenth value is your answer. The tenth value is 19.7; therefore, the car that traveled 19.7 miles per gallon of gasoline is in the 90th percentile, and 90 percent of the cars in your study were less gas efficient.

In summary, you will have to decide which technique works best for your type of data. You can usually express your results in terms of either standard mathematical or statistical graphing. However, there are occasions when only one type will work. If you are dealing with numerous figures or classes of figures, a statistical graph usually works best. For example, if you wanted to demonstrate the variation of test scores between boys and girls in the eighth grade, you would probably make your point clearer by using the statistical method, which would allow you to find the percentiles in which each student scored and the mean test score. On the other hand, if you were investigating the mineral composition of water, the best way to represent the proportion of its contents might be through a pie chart.

Other Means for Representing Data

Since every project is different you may find that you will need other means for showing and explaining your data results. For example, if you need to refer to various stages of a science project experiment that was conducted over a long period of time where measurements may have been taken at various stages at specific times, a **time line** might be a better means of representing your data (see the diagram below). Additionally, if you need to describe the results of a repeated process or a sequence and it is cumbersome to do so through text, a series of **flow charts** may be useful and may make your project data results visually interesting (see the example on the following page).

GROWTH RATE OF AGROBACTERIUM TUMEFACIENS INFECTED PLANT TREATED WITH A BETA-CAROTENE/WATER SOLUTION OVER A 2 MONTH PERIOD OF TIME

first treatment — May 1st
bud appears — May 11th
second bud appears — May 13th
leaves sprout from buds — May 31st
plant has begun to heal in wound area — June 13th
more healing in wound area — June 20th
third bud appears — June 22nd
fourth bud appears — June 24th
plant has grown 2 in. — June 30th

Do Household Sinks Harbor Antibiotic Bacteria?

Choose sink to test

↓

Rub a sterile applicator across surface of sink and then onto petri dish and incubate for 48 hours

↓

Bacteria present? — NO →

↓ YES

Apply filter paper disk soaked in liquid antibiotic and incubate for 48 hours

↓

Check for zone of inhibition

↓

Is there a zone of inhibition? — NO →

↓ YES

Record results (NO branch)   **Record results**   **Bacteria antibiotic resistant**

↓

Bacteria negative or not antibiotic resistant

Summary

1. Data are groups of figures or results you recorded from conducting your experiment. They are organized for observation and drawing conclusions about your experiment.

2. The tabular, graphic, and statistical methods are some of the basic ways of calculating and presenting data.

3. Some basic ways to show your data so that others can see your results at a glance are through the use of line graphs, pie charts, bar graphs, time lines, and flow charts.

6

THE DISPLAY: PUTTING IT ALL TOGETHER FOR THE FAIR

The display is an essential part of your project. Although it alone will not save a bad project, it can enhance the success of a good one. There is nothing more disappointing than to have a judge or viewer overlook a meritorious project purely on the basis of its illegible or disorganized display. Therefore, it is worth spending some extra time making an attractive display.

Due to the guidelines established by the Intel ISEF, most state and regional fairs have put the emphasis on a "poster session" approach, where the backboard is the focal point of the display accompanied by a report and abstract. In general, your display should consist of a great-looking backboard and report both containing text, tables, graphs, charts, photographs, and diagrams to fully illustrate and explain your project.

Your exhibit should show all aspects of your project. There are many ways to do this, but you must remember that all information on the backboard should be clearly and concisely summarized to allow the viewer to grasp the essence of the project quickly. Lengthy discussions should be confined to the report. Only certain items from your project can be displayed. See "Display Restrictions" in this chapter for a general list of what can and cannot be displayed at the science fair.

The Backboard

The backboard is usually the most important part of your display. It should include all the major parts of your project. The backboard is essentially an upright, self-supporting board with organized highlights of your project. It is usually three-sided, although it does not necessarily have to be. The backboard should meet the spacing standards of the Intel ISEF if you plan to enter your project in a state or regional fair that is affiliated with the ISEF. The dimensions of your display must not be more than 108 inches (274 centimeters) high, including the table; 30 inches (76 centimeters) deep, and 48 inches (122 centimeters) wide. If these dimensions are exceeded, you may be disqualified.

When constructing your backboard, stay away from thin posterboard or cardboard. Backboards made of these materials will bend and do not look very professional. Instead, purchase a firm, self-supporting material such as a reinforced paperboard or corkboard. In the long run, you will find these types of

Most state and regional fairs have put emphasis on a "poster session" approach where the backboard is the focal point of the display.

materials easier to work with and more attractive. Alternatively, you may choose to purchase a premade backboard. In recent years this has become a popular choice among students. Two companies that specialize in the sale of premade backboards are *Showboard* and *Science Fair Supply*. Both offer backboards in a variety of sizes and materials and even offer other project display accessories. You can reach Showboard at 1-800-323-9189 or visit their Web site: www.showboard.com. Science Fair Supply can be reached at 1-800-556-3247 or online at: www.sciencefairsupply.com.

Select appropriate lettering for your backboard. Use your computer's word processor or purchase graphic design software that allows you to make a neat, attractive presentation on your backboard. If you do not have software that will allow you to do this, you might want to purchase self-sticking letters or make use of the services of a professional printer. In recent years, almost all science fair project backboards (at the state and international level) have typeface styles and background patterns that have been rendered in one of many terrific graphic design software programs. If you do not have such a program on your home computer, your school probably has one. Whichever program you choose, keep in mind that because so many options are available, it is simply unacceptable to handprint your backboard, especially if you are aiming for a top-notch project.

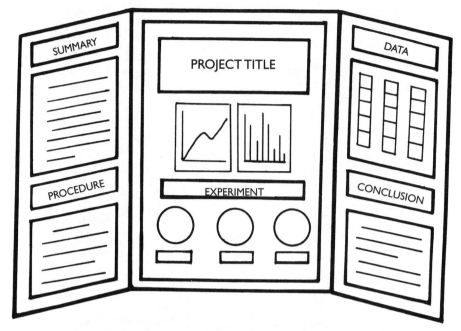

The information on your backboard should be placed in an orderly fashion from left to right under organized headings.

Now that you know how to construct a backboard, you need to know what information you should put on it and where to place it. There is no standard way of making a backboard; however, all the information displayed on it should be well organized. The project title, for example, should stand out in the middle section in bold print. The rest of your information should be placed in an orderly fashion from left to right under organized headings that follow the scientific method. You can also apply headings that relate more specifically to your subject. Whatever headings you choose, make sure they are explicit so that a viewer can grasp each element of your project quickly and efficiently.

The information that you place under each heading is crucial. It must be concise and inclusive. Do not fill up your backboard with excess information. Try to summarize the facts under each heading in no more than 300 words. Additional backboard space can be filled with additional visual information on your subject.

The Report

It is also important that your report be of good quality. This means that you must organize a portfolio of clearly stated, factual information. It is important to keep this in mind because the report is essentially your spokesperson when you are not with your project (for example, during preliminary judging).

An organized report contains the historical background on your subject, an introduction that states your purpose, a procedure that explains your means of acquiring information, your plan for organizing an experiment, and all the recorded data, diagrams, flow charts, photos, conclusions, and other details that fully explain

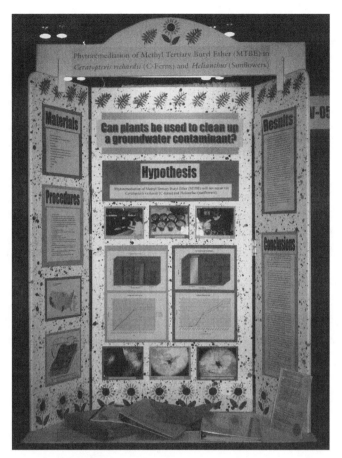

Your backboard should be neat and contain pertinent information laid out in an orderly fashion from left to right under organized headings, including graphs and photographs.

your project. You might even want to include detailed descriptions about different phases in your experiment in the form of a diary. It is a good idea to include the names and places you have visited, together with any related correspondence.

Your report may be easier to complete if you create a journal when you begin to work on your project. If you record everything in your journal as you go along, all you will need to do later is organize your notes, since your journal is essentially the foundation of your report.

In organizing your report, you will have to distinguish between primary and secondary sources of information. Primary sources of information consist of surveys, observations, and experimentation that you have done either alone or through a mentor. Secondary sources are outside sources, such as the library, media organizations, government agencies, companies, laboratories, and so on. If you have used secondary sources for information either quoted directly or used indirectly, you must acknowledge these sources in footnotes and in a bibliography. Also, if you have worked under the guidance of a mentor or adviser be sure to give credit to this person and those who have assisted you in a references section in the report.

As with your backboard, make sure you prepare the report with word processing software on your computer. Never handprint the report. A report will not be able to explain your project as well as you can, but it is reassuring to know that an organized report can work well for you in your absence.

If you write a thorough report that encompasses all of the items mentioned here, you may be eligible to submit it to another type of science competition, such as the Intel Science Talent Search, a local Junior Science and Humanities Symposium, or another similar competition. For more information on these types of science competitions, see Appendix E.

The Abstract

An abstract is a brief summary of your project that is 250–300 words long. The abstract briefly explains the project's purpose and procedural plan and presents generalized data and a short discussion of your conclusions. There is no standard way to write an abstract, but it should always be concise and clear. Many state and regional fairs have made the abstract a mandatory part of science fair project competition and specify that it must be completed and submitted to the science fair's Scientific Review Committee with an application for admission to the science fair. Many science fairs review the abstract to make sure that the project you

Abstract

Is Synthetic Motor Oil Spillage Environmentally Safer than Petroleum Motor Oil Spillage?

The impact of oil spillage is a great concern for the environment whether it be due to its regulated disposal or by accident. The purpose of this project is to determine, in the event of spillage, which form of motor oil, namely, regular petroleum motor oil or synthetic motor oil, would have the least negative impact on the environment. It was hypothesized that the regular petroleum motor oil would have the least negative impact since the synthetic motor oil contains man-made polymers. In order to test this theory, the growth rate of bean plants grown in soil containing traces of unused synthetic motor oil that was administered in various amounts and the growth rate of bean plants grown in the same soil containing traces of unused regular petroleum motor oil that was administered in the same amounts were compared against bean plants that were grown in the same soil where no traces of either type of oil were administered. The results indicated that every bean plant exposed to traces of oil was negatively impacted compared to the control group of bean plants. However, between the two types of oils studied herein, it was evident that the synthetic oil had more of a negative impact upon the plants as evidenced by retarded root length and the ability of the plants to sprout beans which were measured and recorded at various intervals and at the conclusion of the experiment. Therefore, my hypothesis was correct, the spillage of regular petroleum motor oil appears to have the least negative impact.

have been working on meets the standards proscribed by the fair's Scientific Review Committee and the rules and regulations established by that science fair. The abstract further helps to categorize your project into the correct scientific category of competition, and it helps the judges to quickly grasp the summary of your project. It may even suggest to the judges that they should consider your work for other awards that are sponsored by outside special awards presenters.

The previous page contains a simple abstract of a recent award-winning science fair project to give you an idea of how an abstract is written.

Display Restrictions

You read in Chapter 3 about the project limitation guidelines established by the Intel ISEF. The Intel ISEF also has strict regulations involving the exhibition of certain articles in conjunction with the rest of your exhibit. The following is a

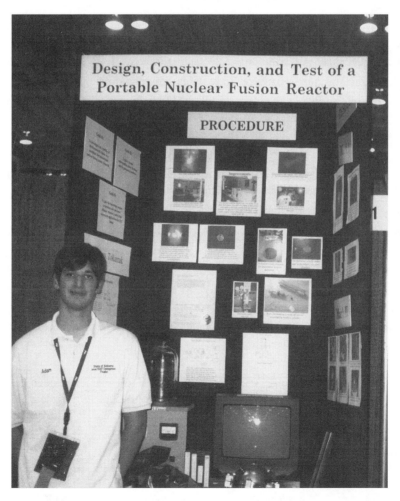

Safety restrictions may prevent you from displaying certain items. The best way to uphold these regulations and explain your project is through the use of photographs, drawings, and charts.

summary of the Intel ISEF display and safety rules. If you have any questions, contact your science fair administrator or Science Service, the organization that administers the Intel ISEF, for more information about what is acceptable for display.

A rule of thumb is to avoid anything that could be potentially hazardous to display in public. The intent of the rule is to protect other students and the public. You can usually uphold such regulations by using photographs, drawings, graphs, charts, and model simulations (where permissible) to show the results of your investigation and research.

If you have any doubts about displaying any part of your project, be sure to first check with officials from your local science fair or contact the Intel ISEF. The following is a summary of items that cannot be displayed.

Items That Cannot Be Displayed

1. Live animals, living organisms, preserved vertebrate/invertebrate animals, taxidermy specimens, or parts including embryos

2. All live materials, including plants and microbes

3. Human or animal parts or body fluids (i.e., blood or urine) except teeth, hair, nails, histological dry mount sections, and wet mount tissue slides properly acquired

4. All soil and waste samples and related materials

5. All chemicals including water and their containers

6. Poisons, drugs, controlled substances, or hazardous substances or devices (e.g., firearms, weapons, ammunition)

7. Food, human or animal

8. Syringes, pipettes, and similar devices and sharp objects

9. Dry ice or other sublimating solids (e.g., solids that can vaporize into a gas without first becoming a liquid)

10. Any flame, open or concealed

11. Highly flammable display materials

12. Tanks that have contained combustible gases or liquids, unless purged with carbon dioxide

13. Batteries with open top cells

14. Photographs and other visual presentations of surgical techniques, dissection, necropsies, and/or laboratory techniques depicting vertebrate animals in other-than-normal conditions

15. Operation of a Class III or IV laser

The following is a summary of items that can be displayed with certain restrictions:

Summary

1. Your science project display is very important and should be presented in an organized and attractive manner.

2. The display should consist of a backboard containing summary information about your project under organized headings that are based on the scientific method, tables, graphs, charts, photographs and diagrams, a report, and an abstract.

3. Backboards must meet the standard space requirements established by the Intel ISEF, which are 108 inches (274 centimeters) high including table, 30 inches (76 centimeters) deep, and 48 inches (122 centimeters) wide.

4. The report can be created primarily from your project journal. It contains all the details about each step in your project along with flow charts and photographs that may be too cumbersome or inappropriate to display on your backboard.

5. An abstract is a short essay that summarizes the goals, methods, and conclusions of your project.

6. The Intel ISEF has established regulations for the restriction and modification of potentially hazardous items for display.

7

AT THE FAIR

This chapter will prepare you for what lies ahead. If you follow the format for completing a project that is recommended in this book, you should be successful. Make sure you have filled out all necessary forms and paperwork and are properly registered as a contestant at your state or regional science fair. This also involves getting your project listed in the correct category of competition.

There are basically two broad categories under which the majority of science fair projects can be categorized—**biological sciences** and **physical sciences.** There are many disciplines within each of these categories, and all of them are further distinguished at most science fairs by grade and by individual entrants or team entrants. The Intel ISEF breaks these categories down into the following scientific disciplines: the biological sciences category consists of projects that pertain to the life sciences—*behavioral and social sciences, biochemistry, botany, gerontology, medicine and health, microbiology,* and *zoology.*

The physical sciences category consists of projects that pertain to *chemistry, computer science, earth and space science, engineering, environmental science, mathematics,* and *physics.*

It is usually easy to determine the category where your project belongs, but sometimes it may be difficult. For example, if you did a project on human prosthetic limbs and joints, in which you studied the physics of how artificial joints wear after a period of time, in what category would your project belong? Well, if your project emphasized the amount of friction in a joint, it would probably be a physical sciences project. But if you began to discuss the biodegradability of the device, your project might be more appropriately placed in the biological sciences category. The wrong choice could hurt your outcome in the competition.

Setting Up Your Project

As you set up your project, pay careful attention to the space requirements mentioned in Chapter 6 (the space should be marked off). Your backboard and display should be self-supporting, but it is wise to bring spray mount, a stapler, glue, tape, and an extension cord (if applicable to your display) in case your project needs minor repairs or modifications.

After your project is completely set up, a fair representative will check it to make sure everything complies with the fair rules and safety regulations. Make sure that you have everything displayed properly and have any necessary instructions available for the fair staff or judges (this is especially important if you have a project that involves the use of a computer or some other type of mechanically operated display).

Judging at the State and Regional Fair

At some fairs, judging takes place as soon as all the projects are set up. Students and parents are not allowed in the exhibit hall during this time. Generally, judges are assigned to separate divisions as teams. They begin by reviewing the projects in their category individually and then as a group, in which they exchange thoughts with team members and rank the projects. While judging systems vary from science fair to science fair, typically, most state and regional fairs will spend one day on this type of preliminary judging in which they determine those projects that rank in the top 25–50%. These projects then qualify to compete for the second round of judging which is referred to as final judging. This final round determines place awards and eligibility of the best projects in grades 9–12 for the Intel ISEF.

During the final round of judging, state and regional science fair contestants who have made the first round cut (finalists) are invited to give an oral presentation for a variety of judges. The judges may represent the fair itself, professional and academic associations, or business that distribute specialized awards.

Most state and regional science fair judges score contestants on various criteria, including:

1. *Scientific approach to the problem/engineering goals.* This is often the most important and substantial criterion that is judged. This criterion measures whether the exhibitor shows evidence of applied scientific skill or engineering development through recognizing the scope and limitation of the issue that is being studied and addressing the scope of the problem including the quality of the work, time spent securing data, and whether the exhibitor's observations support this data.

2. *Creative ability/originality.* This criterion also weighs substantially in the exhibitor's score and basically measures the ingenuity and originality of the problem that is being studied and/or in the exhibitor's approach to the problem. Judges look for whether you have chosen the best method possible in your investigation and whether you have made the most effective use of materials, equipment, and techniques pertaining to your topic. They also take into account whether your project is unique, how you derived your topic, and credit you give to mentors who may have assisted you.

3. *Thoroughness and accuracy.* This area measures the depth of the literature used concerning the project as well as the quality of the experimental investigation and your use and analysis of data results.

4. *Clarity.* This criterion determines whether the project's scope, purpose, or goals are clear and concise. Exhibitors sometimes get swept away by the

At most science and regional fairs, contestants are asked to give several presentations for both fair and special award judges from different organizations and businesses.

complexity of their subject and fail to communicate their project's purpose to the judges. While it is admirable to acquire a new scientific or technical lingo while pursuing your topic, you will not impress anyone if you fail to communicate the topic clearly and concisely.

5. *Advancement of exhibitor's knowledge in science.* This area looks at whether the student has a good handle and understanding of the primary aspects that concern his or her topic, which includes both basic research and experimental principles.

6. *Other.* Some science fairs also grade your exhibit partly on its dramatic value—i.e., whether it is presented in a way that has visual appeal through the use of graphics, and workmanship. To the extent that you may be working with a partner on a team science fair project, an additional part of your overall score may include points on how the project was handled by the team, management, delegation and sharing of workload, expertise of each team member, and so on.

Keep in mind that judging is a difficult task that requires the skill and expertise of a wide range of qualified professionals. The judges are analyzing the overall quality of work that has been done on a subject matter that involves probing, testing, and reasoning in a creative sense. They are not interested in plain library research resembling a book report, meaningless collections, or copied work from books or other science fair projects that have been completed in previous years.

Presenting Your Project in an Interview

If you become a finalist, you will have the opportunity to be present with your project during judging, which is an enviable position. You will be able to explain in detail the research, procedures, methods, and conclusions in your project. Practice what you are going to say before the fair, so that your presentation will be smooth and relaxed. If possible, have your mentor, teacher, or someone familiar with your project interview you by asking you key questions that will likely be asked during judging.

Above all, the key is to be so well versed on your subject matter that you can handle any random questions that come your way. Judges want to see that you understand your project thoroughly and that you actually did the work yourself. They do not want to hear a memorized presentation that sounds like you are reciting a script. They want to be able to interject and ask you questions so they can see that you are thinking on your feet. They want to understand exactly what it is that you did and what you accomplished. If you cannot get these points across to a judge, you are not going to fare well, even if you conducted the most sophisticated experiment on the most interesting topic and achieved the most amazing results. None of this will matter if you do not communicate well to the judges. By being prepared to properly handle any question that might come your way, you will score very well with the judges.

The following is a list of the main questions you should be prepared to answer when you are presenting your project to a judge.

The Main Questions You Need to Be Able to Answer about Your Project

1. What is your project about?
2. Why did you select this project?
3. What did you expect to accomplish with your project?
4. Why did you choose the experiment that you did, and did it provide the answers to what you were seeking?
5. What was your experimental plan, how did you gather your data, and can you explain the data you obtained? (Be prepared to use your display as a visual aid.)
6. Was this the best experiment to achieve your goal?
7. What conclusions have you drawn from this project, and what might be done to further your investigation in this project?

Remember, every now and then a judge will ask a question that no one could have anticipated and you may not have the answer for. If this happens to you, do not panic. Sometimes judges test you to see if you really did the work yourself and if you really have a handle on the subject matter of your project. While you should be able to answer anything about your project that you have on your backboard and in your report or abstract, you might be surprised by this type of trick question. If you find yourself in this situation, just explain to the judge that because your project covered so many different aspects of the topic you do not recall at the present time the answer to that particular question. You can also state that while you do not have the answer, you will certainly look into the question that was raised. Alternately, offer the judge an explanation on something related to this line of questioning that you might be familiar with (if you can do so), or just state that you are not familiar with the issue he or she is referring to but that you would be glad to inform the judge about another aspect concerning the project that is extremely relevant to the results you achieved.

It is important to realize that science fair judges at the state and regional level are typically experienced scientific researchers, engineers, mathematicians, doctors, and professors and are quite capable of detecting any errors or "fake" experimental results. They will also be able to tell if you just memorized your presentation or whether someone else did the work for you and if you do not have a working knowledge of your subject. Those individuals were selected as judges because they have a high level of expertise in a particular scientific discipline, which may incidentally be the category in which your project is entered at the fair. Also, be aware that the judge may have already seen a project similar to yours at another science fair.

Judging usually takes from a few hours to a full day with breakout sessions for lunch and workshops. Try to be consistent with every judge interviewing you; stay alert, and concentrate on what you want to say even though you may have already said the same thing to the last judge. If you must leave your project momentarily, leave a note stating that you will return soon. General tips to keep in mind for a successful presentation are: know your material, be thorough, be confident, communicate well, and enjoy a wonderful experience!

And the Winner Is . . .

After final judging, scores are tallied and the winners in each division are announced. The top high school projects of an Intel ISEF–affiliated state or regional fair qualify for competition in the Intel ISEF. Simply making it to the state or regional fair is an honor, but only a few can experience the prestige of participating in the Intel ISEF. Please see Chapter 1 for more information about this competition and Appendix E about alternative science fair project competitions.

Specialized Awards

Some science fairs include special areas of competition that are separate from the general fair honors. These special categories are accessible to students who complete a project concentrated in a particular area of science. Various companies and organizations present special awards. These groups honor excellence in a subject area related to the particular field that their organization specializes in, and these awards sometimes consist of prestigious scholarships, grants, and internships.

Closing Notes

This book was written to alleviate the frustration that often arises when students begin a science fair project. It attempts to explain the strategies and secrets often used by top winners. Although this book cannot guarantee that you will make it to the top with your science fair project, it can improve your chances and increase your motivation for future success. Chances are good that your achievement will be recognized by college and business recruiters who are looking for science talent and dedication. Remember, many of today's respected scientists, engineers, doctors, and college professors began their careers by participating in science fairs. You, too, can follow in their footsteps by investing your time and talent in a science fair project.

Summary

1. It is important to check with your teacher or science fair officials to register your project properly and on time in the correct science fair category and division.

2. There are two broad categories under which the majority of science fair projects can be categorized—**biological sciences** and **physical sciences.** There are many disciplines within each category and all of them are further distinguished at most science fairs by grade and by individual entrants or team entrants.

3. While judging systems vary from science fair to science fair, most state and regional fairs typically spend one day on preliminary judging where those projects that rank in the top 25–50 percent are determined. These projects qualify to compete for the second round of judging, which is referred to as final judging.

4. Most state and regional science fair judges score contestants on these five basic criteria:
   a. Scientific approach to the problem/engineering goals
   b. Creative ability/originality
   c. Thoroughness and accuracy
   d. Clarity
   e. Advancement of the exhibitor's knowledge in science

5. In order to do well presenting your project to a judge, try to be so well-versed on your subject matter that you can handle any random questions that come your way.

PART
II

35 Award-Winning
Science Fair Projects

Important Notes Before You Begin

The following pages contain outline samples for 35 award-winning science fair projects. The summaries and diagrams should help to advise you on how to prepare your project, particularly if you are a first-time science fair participant. These outlines are not intended to do the work for you but to provide you with a variety of useful models to follow. The results of these 35 projects have thus been eliminated, and lists of questions have been prepared instead, so that you may have a guide for drawing conclusions about the projects. The summary of one International Science and Engineering Fair project (Project #13) is included in order to give you a sense of the caliber that is required for this highest level of competition.

As you read through these projects, you may require information about where to obtain some of the scientific equipment mentioned in the experiments. Refer to Appendix C for a list of scientific supply companies from which laboratory equipment and other supplies may be purchased in your area.

Finally, you should keep in mind that the project outlines come from a variety of scientific disciplines and require minimal to advanced levels of scientific skill. They were developed by actual students in grades 7 through 12 and do not come from a lab workbook. Thus, there is no guarantee that any of the experimental procedures for any project will work as the experiment may indicate. The outlines represent award-winning work on different grade levels. Therefore, while students with little scientific experience may find some of the projects difficult, they should find others particularly suitable. Where noted, the assistance of a research scientist is required or precautions must be taken, and special skills are needed for certain projects. Be sure to heed these notices. They are there for your safety and to let you know whether or not a particular project is for you. In addition, check with your science fair project adviser for further guidance and safety precautions before starting any project appearing in this book. Most importantly, exercise common sense and good judgment when conducting any science experiment.

Does the Composition of Rosin Affect the Sound a Violin Produces?

Note: Prior knowledge of musical notes and the ability to hear and detect them is helpful in conducting this experiment.

Purpose

To investigate if there is a difference in sound quality between different types of violin rosins when applied to the bow of a violin and the violin itself.

Hypothesis

Even though oil of turpentine is the principal ingredient in all rosins, every rosin manufacturer uses different raw materials. Thus if various manufactured rosins are made from different materials, then each will have a different effect on the sound a violin produces when applied to a violin bow.

Materials Needed

- violin rosins by various manufacturers, for example, Bernadel, Hill Dark, Hill Light, L'Opera Jade, and Pirastro Goldflex
- 2 carbon graphite bows
- microphone and sound card
- computer with Microsoft Windows Sound Recorder software
- violin
- Digital Orchestrator Pro software for sound wave comparison
- unused violin bow horsehair strands
- 30x microscope

Experiment

In the first part of the experiment, various brands of rosin will be applied separately to a violin bow. The bow will then be used to play a particular note on the violin after being treated with a specific brand of rosin. The results will be picked up by a microphone and sound card attached to a computer and recorded in a computer program that will display sound waves of each rosin-treated bow. In the second part of the experiment, horsehairs will be treated individually with the same rosin brands used in the sound recording part of the procedure, and their physical shape will be observed under a 30x microscope.

Procedure

Phase 1

1. Choose one brand of violin rosin and apply it to the bow.
2. Plug the microphone into the line-in jack (located on the sound card) on the back of the computer.
3. Turn the computer on and open the program called Sound Recorder.
4. Open the File menu, then open the Properties menu, click on "Convert Now," click on "CD Quality," and click "OK" twice.
5. Move the microphone six inches away from the instrument's bridge.
6. Click "Record."
7. Pick up the violin and play the A-string for fifteen seconds at a rate of one bow stroke per second.

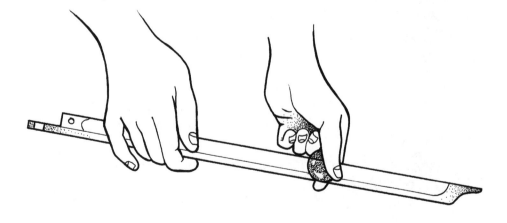

Each brand of rosin will be applied separately to the bow for testing.

Once you have applied a rosin to the bow, open up the sound recording software program on your computer and turn on the microphone. Pick up the violin and play the A string. Record the sound waves created from stroking the rosin treated bow on this string.

8. Click "Stop" and save the recording as a file under the name of the brand of rosin being tested.

9. After recording the sound from the violin, clean the rosin off the bow by sweeping the bow back and forth across a clean cloth.

10. Once the bow is thoroughly clean, apply the second brand of rosin to the bow.

11. Repeat steps 5–9 for all remaining brands of rosin.

12. When finished, perform the experiment from the beginning for two more trials to ensure accurate and consistent data results. Then repeat the entire experiment with the second bow.

13. When finished gathering data, open the sound recording files you created in the computer program called Digital Orchestrator Pro, and observe your data. Your files will be viewable as sound wave patterns that should be printed and collected for your data analysis.

Phase 2

1. Observe the horsehair strands under the 30x microscope, and note the physical shape of each horsehair. If possible, take a photograph of what you see with a special microscope camera.

2. Apply each brand of rosin to a different strand of horsehair previously viewed under the microscope. Apply the rosin about ten times back and forth.

3. Examine each strand again under the 30x microscope and note the physical shape of each horsehair containing each particular brand of rosin and record your data.

Results

1. Look at the sound wave patterns for each rosin tested and for each trial of the experiment with the same rosin for the first bow. Then look at the sound wave patterns for each rosin tested and for each trial of the experiment with the same rosin for the second bow. Are the results consistent for each trial of each brand of rosin? Were the results consistent between the different trials and between the two bows for the same brand of rosin? If not, what may have accounted for variations in your results?

2. If you received consistent results, compare the crests and troughs among the sound wave pattern results for each rosin tested. Were different sound waves recorded for each different type of rosin tested?

3. Look at the results of the physical appearances of the horsehairs, both before they were treated with different brands of rosin and after, that you obtained from under the microscope. Can you see the fine details of any of the horsehairs treated with the various brands of rosin? Are any of the strands thicker? Do any of the treated strands reflect light?

4. Are there any correlations between the physical structure of a horsehair treated with a particular brand of rosin and the sound quality produced by a violin whose bow was treated with the same rosin? For example, if a brand of rosin appears to thicken a horsehair, does this influence the size of the crests and troughs in the sound patterns?

Discovery Channel Young Scientist Challenge and Connecticut Science Fair finalist Jonathan Sellon and his project.

2

A Hare-Raising Experience: Do Mendel's Theories on Heredity Apply to Rabbits?

Note: Check with your teacher or science fair adviser for appropriate forms and permission to work on this project because strict rules apply to experiments involving vertebrate animals. You are required to complete additional forms for the prescreening of your project and approval by a scientific review committee authorized by your state or regional science fair before you start your research.

Purpose

To determine if two rabbits with the same hair/coat color will pass the same hair/coat color to their offspring, which color traits are dominant, and whether or not coat color can be specifically predicted using Mendel's theory of heredity.

Hypothesis

In the 1800s, Gregor Mendel, the father of genetics, theorized that different trait characteristics always appeared to be either dominant or recessive as applied to offspring. He further noted that each trait characteristic was inherited independently and that each trait characteristic was determined by a dominant or recessive gene factor from each parent for that characteristic. If such theories apply to all characteristics of all living things, then the coat color of the offspring of two rabbits of the same breed should be predicted once the dominant and recessive coat color characteristics carried by each parent rabbit are identified.

Materials Needed

- Two Jersey Wooly pedigree rabbits (or other available pedigree breed), one male and one female that are exactly the same color and have had at least one litter together (that is available to study), or are expecting a litter. Plan to work with a breeder or veterinarian who knows how to provide proper care for the rabbits, including food, shelter, and medical care, especially if the female rabbit is expecting a litter.

- Pedigrees for the two rabbits (a pedigree is a document that provides the ancestry for an animal). For a rabbit, a pedigree will usually provide the name of the sire (father) and the dam (mother), followed by the sires and dams for the father and mother of these rabbits and so on. You will also find the breed type, sex, date of birth, and other information.

- Book or chart containing rabbit hair/coat color gene types—for example, *The ABCs of Rabbit Coat Colors* by Glenna Huffmon.

- Large sheets of paper for making a family tree and creating a Punnet square (an offspring genetic trait prediction chart produced by matching all gene types present for a particular characteristic between the mother and father). The gene types should be represented by a pair of letters with an uppercase letter representing the dominant forms, and a lowercase letter representing the recessive forms. You can find these combinations and how to interpret them in a book or chart containing rabbit hair/coat color gene types, such as *The ABCs of Rabbit Coat Colors* by Glenna Huffmon.

Experiment

The color of the hair/coats of the offspring of a male and a female rabbit of the exact same color and of the exact same breed will be compared with predictions made from possible gene type combinations developed using a Punnett square with gene type combinations obtained from the pedigree certificates of the two rabbits.

Procedure

1. Research all possible hair/coat colors for the rabbit breed you are working with and note them in a journal.

2. Using the pedigrees of the two rabbits you are working with, make a family tree and carefully note the coat colors of all ancestors and compare them to the coat colors noted for that particular breed.

3. Prepare a Punnet square or an offspring prediction chart noting all hair/coat color gene type combinations that are possible between your two rabbits. Place all possible sire gene combinations down the side of the chart and all possible gene combinations from the dam across the top of the chart. Then match each gene combination of the sire with that of the dam and note the predicted outcome of hair/coat color for an offspring receiving that particu-

Male Pedigree

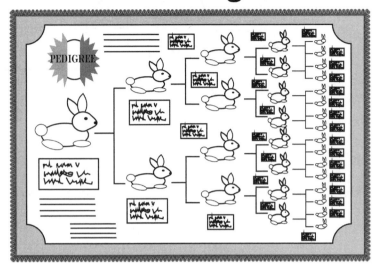

Female Pedigree

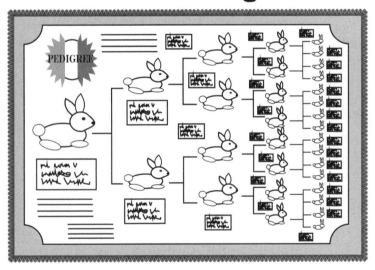

A pedigree is a document that provides the ancestry of a rabbit. You will need to obtain the pedigrees for your test rabbits and make a family tree noting the coat colors of the rabbits' ancestors.

lar combination. Note which combinations are more probable than others, and therefore what hair/coat color appears to be the most likely outcome of their litter.

4. Observe the litter of your two rabbits and compare them with the results you predicted in your chart.

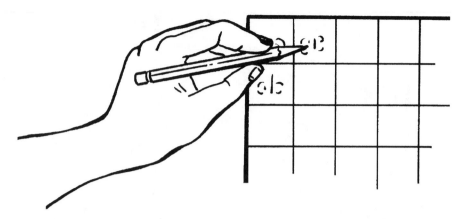

Create a Punnet Square by matching all hair/coat color combinations for your pair of rabbits.

Results

1. Are the colors of the offspring's hair/coats exactly the same as the parents or did different color combinations show up from ancestors as shown in your prediction charts? Does this suggest that rabbit coat color is a trait characteristic that can be readily estimated using a prediction chart or is it purely random?

2. Was the color of the parent rabbits considered dominant or recessive based on your research?

3. Which hair/coat colors appeared most frequently? Are the colors that appeared most frequently also considered genetically dominant among the breed? What genes would need to be present in order to create a litter of the same hair/color?

3

Heat of
Reaction

Purpose

To determine if heat will be released or absorbed during certain acid/base chemical reactions.

Hypothesis

Heat of reaction is the quantity of heat released or absorbed in a chemical reaction. Water (a neutral substance) has a specific heat capacity of one unit. The specific heat capacities of other substances are different but bear a constant ratio to that of water. Therefore, if adding room temperature water to room temperature water results in no measurable amount of heat being released or absorbed, then it is possible that adding different strengths of room temperature acids and bases to room temperature water may react in such a way that a measurable amount of heat may be released or absorbed.

Materials Needed

Note: All materials must be at room temperature

- 3 beakers (600 ml each)
- distilled water (1 liter)
- TI thermometer
- whole milk (200 ml)
- household ammonia (200 ml)
- squeezed lemon juice (200 ml)
- liquid antacid (200 ml)

- 100% grapefruit juice (200 ml)
- baking soda (200 ml)
- triple beam balance
- chemistry or physics textbook containing the specific heat capacities for the acids and bases tested

Experiment

Five variables consisting of acid and base combinations—weak acid + strong base, strong acid + weak base, medium acid + medium base, weak acid + weak base, and strong acid + strong base—will be added separately to distilled water (the purpose of which is to provide a constant temperature environment for the acids and bases being tested) and will be tested for the quantity of heat released or absorbed by their combinations.

Procedures

1. Place 200 ml of distilled water into one beaker (beaker 1), insert the thermometer and stir until a constant temperature is reached, measure the temperature in degrees Celsius and record the temperature (should be at or around room temperature).

2. The first reaction will be completed with milk and ammonia (weak acid and strong base). Place 100 ml of milk into beaker 2. Place 100 ml of ammonia into beaker # 3. Insert the thermometer into the milk and stir until a constant temperature is reached, measure the temperature in degrees Celsius, and record the temperature (should be at or around room temperature). Do the same for beaker 3 containing the ammonia. Then, pour beaker 2 and beaker 3 into beaker 1 at the same time. Insert the thermometer into beaker 1 and stir until the solution is evenly distributed throughout while recording the temperature every 2 seconds for a total period of 20 seconds.

Various combinations of acids and bases will be added to a beaker of water to determine the total heat released or absorbed during each chemical reaction.

3. Pour all the liquids out and clean the beakers.

4. Start the second reaction (strong acid and weak base) with the squeezed lemon juice and liquid antacid. Repeat steps 1 and 2.

5. Start the third reaction (medium acid and medium base) with the grapefruit juice and baking soda. Repeat steps 1 and 2.

6. Start the fourth reaction (weak acid and weak base) with the milk and antacid. Repeat steps 1–2.

7. Start the fifth reaction (strong acid and strong base) with the lemon juice and ammonia. Repeat steps 1–2.

8. Collect all of your data and organize them in a table.

9. Calculate the temperature changes in each of the five solutions.

10. Find the mass in grams using your balance scale for each reaction (2 solutions + water).

11. Once you have gathered your data from steps 9–10, you can then calculate the total heat released or absorbed during each chemical reaction. The total heat is calculated using this formula:

> Total heat = specific heat capacity (J/g °C) × mass (grams) × the difference in temperature (°C)

Note: The specific heat capacity of a substance is the quantity of heat required to increase the temperature of unit mass of the substance by one degree. Specific heat capacity for liquids is a constant that can typically be found in a chemistry or physics textbook.

Results

1. What was the total heat of each reaction?

2. Was heat absorbed or released in each reaction?

3. Does a stronger acid or a stronger base correlate to heat being absorbed or released in the reaction? Does a weaker acid or weaker base correlate to heat being absorbed or released in the reaction?

4. What practical applications would this experiment have for industry?

4

A Study and Comparison of the Quantity and Potency of Antioxidents among Various Teas

Note: This project uses materials and equipment found in a biochemistry laboratory. The student will need to work with a mentor who is a biochemistry research scientist or graduate student who can assist with performing certain procedures and operating various types of equipment.

Purpose

To determine the amount of antioxidants present in various teas and compare the concentration of antioxidants of the first flush of tea to two subsequent flushes with the same tea leaves or tea bag.

Hypothesis

Free radicals have been known to cause a multitude of health problems and diseases through cell damage and the disturbance of DNA. Free radicals are atoms or groups of atoms with one or more (unpaired) electrons. Antioxidants, conversely, are molecules that can safely interact with free radicals and end their cumulative destruction before vital molecules are damaged—by donating electrons to the unpaired electrons found in the free radicals. Tea is believed to contain a large amount of antioxidants, and people in some cultures believe that subsequent flushes with the same tea leaves or tea bag are more beneficial to one's health. This project will test the validity of these beliefs.

Materials Needed

- green tea, oolong, and black tea bags/leaves
- beakers
- distilled water
- hot plate
- Fisher™ p8 filter paper
- pipettes
- ethanol
- F-C reagent
- 2% $NaCo_3$ solution
- warm water bath
- gallic acid

Instruments Needed

- UV/Visible spectrophotometer

Experiment

Tea samples will be prepared and tested for antioxidant presence. Initially, the total amount of polyphenols present in each tea sample will be determined. (Polyphenols are naturally occurring chemical compounds that are powerful antioxidants. In tea, the primary polyphenols are called catechins. Other polyphenols found in tea include flavanols, flavanol glycosides, flavandiols, phenolic acids, and depsides.) This will be done using the Folin-Ciocalten assay test. A UV/visible spectrometer will be used for absorbance measurements to determine the amount of antioxidant in each sample.

Procedure

The Folin-Ciocalten (F-C) assay test for determining total amount of polyphenols in each tea sample.

1. Choose one of the teas to be studied. Pour a measured amount of loose tea leaves or place a tea bag (of this particular type of tea) into a beaker and then pour in 100mL of boiling distilled water. Cover, and after 5 minutes separate the tea from the tea bag or from the tea leaves by filtering it through p8 filter paper. Repeat this procedure two more times with the same tea leaves or tea bag to obtain a total of three flush samples.

2. In a clean beaker, take the pipettes and dilute 0.27ml tea extract solution from step 1 in 15.63 ml water, 0.1 ml ethanol, 1.00 ml F-C reagent, and 3.00 ml 2% $NaCO_3$ to make a total of 20.00 ml. Heat at 50°C in a water bath for 5 minutes. Determine the absorbance on a UV/visible spectrophotometer at 765 nm. Repeat steps 1–2 two more times using the other flush samples from the same tea leaves or tea bag.

3. Prepare a calibration curve using gallic acid as the standard of phenol at concentrations of 1, 2, 3, 4, 5, × 10^5M. Compare the absorbance of the sample with the calibration curve to obtain the total polyphenol content of each tea sample from the same tea leaves or tea bag.

4. Repeat steps 1–3 with the remaining tea samples.

Results

1. What were the total amounts of polyphenols present in each tea sample after the first flush? What were the total amounts of polyphenols present in each tea sample after the second and third flushes?

2. Which tea type contained the greatest amount of polyphenols after the first flush? After the second flush? After the third flush?

3. Which tea had the greatest concentration of polyphenols overall?

4. Assuming that an increased presence of polyphenols found in tea is beneficial to one's health, which tea and which flush of this tea proved to have the highest concentration of polyphenols?

5

Is There a Correlation between Toilet Paper Texture/Thickness and Low-Flow Toilet Bowl Clogging?

Purpose

To determine if there is a correlation between the brand of toilet paper used and the frequency of low-flow toilet bowl clogging.

Hypothesis

In recent years, toilets have been regulated to allow for a maximum water usage of 1.6 gallons per flush to conserve on water resources. These toilets are referred to as low-flow toilets. While having water-efficient toilets might save homeowners some money on water usage, they might be more costly for them in the long run if the homeowner has to flush multiple times or else deal with frequent clogging. If different types of toilet paper are made of different plies and textures, then they may not all be capable of being flushed completely during an initial flush of a low-flow toilet, and some may actually clog a low-flow toilet. The texture and thickness of toilet paper varies among manufacturers; therefore, there may be some toilet paper brands that do clog or impede the flushing of a low-flow toilet and some that do not.

Materials Needed

- toilet paper of various textures and plies by various manufacturers
- bucket that can hold at least 2 gallons of water
- tap water
- measuring cup
- stopwatch
- distilled water
- low-flow toilet

Experiment

Various brands of toilet paper in various textures and plies will be tested to see which will break down and disintegrate the fastest in a swirling bucket of 1.6 gallons of tap water and then again in a swirling bucket of 1.6 gallons of distilled water (a control to determine if water composition may be a factor). This action is to duplicate that of a low-flow toilet flushing. A stopwatch will record the amount of time it takes to break down and disintegrate one sheet of toilet paper from each of the brands tested.

Procedure

1. Collect several different rolls of toilet paper of different textures, plies, thicknesses, and absorbencies from various manufacturers. Remove a few sheets from each roll, being careful to note the roll from which each sheet was obtained.

2. Measure 1.6 gallons of tap water into the bucket. Place the first sheet of toilet paper that is being tested into the bucket, start the stopwatch, and swirl the water around in the bucket in a continuous motion until the sheet of paper begins to break up into pieces.

3. Stop timing the disintegration of the sheet of toilet paper as soon as it breaks into pieces. Log the disintegration time for the brand.

4. Remove the toilet paper remnants and refill the bucket with enough tap water to ensure that the bucket contains 1.6 gallons of water.

5. Repeat steps 2–4 for all remaining brands of toilet paper.

6. Empty the bucket completely and fill with 1.6 gallons of distilled water.

7. Repeat steps 2–4 with the same brands of toilet paper using the distilled water.

8. Repeat entire experiment at least 5 times to ensure accurate and consistent results for each brand tested.

9. Test your results by gathering about 10 sheets of each toilet paper sample together in a bunch. Place the bunched-up toilet paper in a low-flow toilet and flush. Note the rate and ease with which the toilet flushes and whether you need to flush again to ensure that the paper goes completely down the toilet. Repeat this step for each additional brand of toilet paper and note your results. Compare your results with the results gathered from the sample sheets that were tested in the bucket.

Results

1. How long did it take for each sheet of toilet paper to break apart in the bucket containing tap water? Are the results consistent for each trial for each brand of toilet paper that was tested?

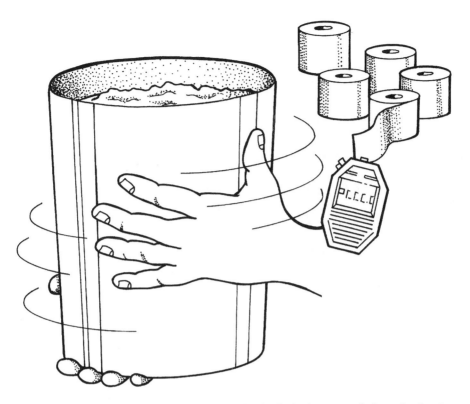

Various types of toilet paper will be tested individually by being swirled in a bucket in a continuous motion and will be timed for how quickly each disintegrates.

2. How long did it take for each sheet of toilet paper to break apart in the bucket containing distilled water? Are the results consistent for each trial for each brand of toilet paper that was tested?

3. Were there variations in the time it took to break down the toilet paper samples between the tap water and the distilled water?

4. Did the brands that broke down the fastest correlate to a thinner texture and ply of toilet paper? Did the brands that broke down the slowest correlate to a thicker texture and ply of toilet paper?

5. Compare the results of the toilet paper that was flushed with the sample sheets that were tested in the buckets of water for each brand. Did the brands that took the least amount of time to break apart take the shortest time to flush? If not, what may account for this? Did the brands that took the longest to break apart take the longest to flush? If not, what may account for this?

6

Which Vegetable Plant Has the Greatest Development of Calluses after Being Cloned?

Purpose

To determine whether carrot, cauliflower, or broccoli has a greater rate of development of calluses when the plants are cloned.

Hypothesis

Plant calluses are important because they are composed of cells from which plant growth can be regenerated. The greater number of calluses present in a plant, the more useful it will be to a grower. Plant cloning helps growers by saving them the time required by the seed germination process of growing, and the genetic code of the best plant can be preserved forever. Therefore, it is hypothesized that if cuttings are taken from different types of plants that are healthy and exhibit strong growth, then clones of these plants may be just as healthy and have more calluses than plants that are not cloned.

Materials Needed

- 15 sterile specimen cups
- sterile distilled water
- 70% ethyl alcohol solution
- 10% bleach solution
- 5 pieces of cauliflower (each from a different head); 5 pieces of carrot (only the inside of the root (1 mm x 1 mm) (each from a different bundle);
- 5 pieces of broccoli (each from a different head)
- beakers
- regular distilled water
- sterile long and short forceps
- beaker containing 100% ethyl alcohol
- Bunsen burner (flame)

- 30 large test tubes of Murashige minimal organic medium
- 15 large test tubes of shoot initiation medium
- 15 peat pots
- soil
- 15 small plastic bags

Experiment

Five cuttings of carrot, cauliflower, and broccoli from different specimens of cauliflower, carrots, and broccoli (to ensure that the results are consistent for each plant being studied) will be sterilized using bleach, ethyl alcohol, and sterile distilled water. They will be put into test tubes of minimal organic medium to produce calluses. After a week in this medium they will be moved to a shoot initiation medium. Once the plants have produced shoots they will be moved into new tubes of minimal organic medium to form roots. The production of the rate of calluses in the plants will be observed and compared.

Procedure

1. Take 10 of the sterile specimen cups and label 6 cups for sterile distilled water, 2 cups for 70% ethyl alcohol, and 2 cups for 10% bleach. Put sterile distilled water into the appropriate cups so that they are about half full. Put 70% ethyl alcohol solution into the appropriate cups so that they are about half full. Make a 10% bleach solution by mixing 90 cc of distilled water with 10 ml of bleach and mix. Fill the cups marked for 10% bleach halfway with this solution.

2. Cut the cauliflower florets into 5 small pieces (about 1 mm x 1 mm) and put them in a beaker of regular distilled water for a minute.

3. Put the 5 pieces of cauliflower florets into the first cup marked sterile distilled water and swirl for 30 seconds. Remove the pieces using sterile forceps. (Sterile forceps should be used each time the cuttings are transported to a different solution and the forceps should be resterilized between the transfer of each piece. To sterilize both the long and short forceps, place the tips in 100% alcohol and then run them through a Bunsen burner flame. Safety precautions for flaming should be taken to prevent burns.)

4. Place the cauliflower pieces into one of the ethyl alcohol cups and swirl for 15 seconds.

5. Then place the cauliflower pieces into another cup of sterile distilled water and swirl for another 30 seconds.

6. Place the pieces of cauliflower into one of the cups containing 10% bleach solution. Leave them in this solution for 25 minutes, swirling approximately every 2 minutes.

7. Put the cauliflower pieces into another cup of sterile distilled water, swirl them with a fast motion, and leave them in the cup for 5 minutes. After 5 minutes, drain the water and then cover the pieces with a small amount of

sterile distilled water. Again, swirl the cup and then leave still for 5 minutes. Repeat this procedure twice.

8. Remove the cauliflower pieces with the long forceps and place each one into an individual test tube filled with Murashige minimal organic medium. Push the cuttings down slightly with the tip of the forceps into the medium. Store the test tubes in a warm, dark area. (Remember to sterilize the forceps in between the transfer of each cutting of cauliflower; the tops of the tubes should be sterilized before and after inserting the pieces of cauliflower into the medium. Do not dip the tops of the medium-holding tubes in alcohol, but run them through the flame before and after inserting the cutting. Safety precautions for flaming should be taken to prevent burns.)

9. Cut the carrots into small slices, then cut the slices around so that only the inside root piece of each carrot slice will be used. Prepare five small pieces of carrot (similar in size to the 1 mm x 1 mm pieces of cauliflower). Repeat steps 2–8 with the carrots.

10. Cut the broccoli florets into 5 small pieces (about 1mm x 1mm) and repeat steps 2–8 with the broccoli.

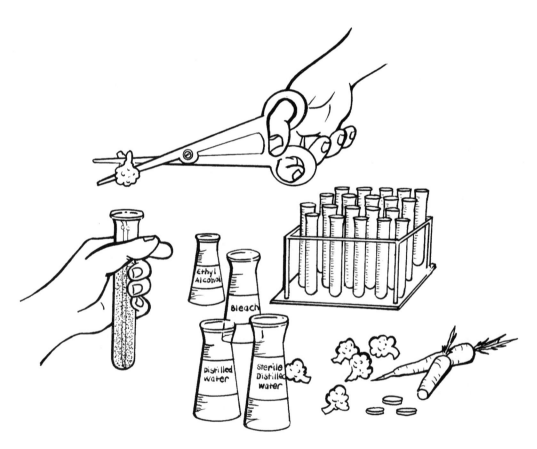

Sterilized cuttings of a sample vegetable being placed into a test tube containing the Murashige minimal organic medium.

11. After the cuttings have been in the Murashige minimal organic medium for one week, transfer them to tubes of the shoot initiation medium using long sterile forceps. Label each cauliflower tube as "cauliflower, 1-5," each carrot tube as "carrot, 1-5," and each broccoli tube as "broccoli, 1-5." Then store the tubes in a dark space for four weeks. Each week note your observations of the progress in each of the tubes to note the formation of shoots and roots.

12. After 4 weeks, transfer the cuttings into new test tubes of the Murashige minimal organic medium. This is for the purpose of fostering root formation. Store the plants in a dark closed-in space. Make observations daily of the progress in each of the tubes, noting the formation of shoots and roots.

13. After one week, the cuttings should be ready to be planted in soil. When planting, it is not necessary to use sterile materials. Simply take the cuttings out from the tubes one at a time and wash them to remove extra bits of medium. Then plant them in premoistened soil in a peat pot. Place a small, clear plastic bag over the peat pot to collect moisture.

14. After the cuttings have been planted for a week, remove the plastic bags for 1 hour on the eighth day. On the following day, remove the bags for $1\frac{1}{2}$ hours. Continue adding a half hour each day until the plants are able to grow on their own. Water as necessary.

15. To determine which plant had a greater production rate of calluses, look at the formation of shoots and roots in the shoot initiation medium and in the Murashige minimal organic medium. If the cutting formed a callus while in the original minimal organic medium, it will then be able to form shoots and roots when transferred to the next two medium tubes. Calluses can also be checked by seeing which plants grow after being put in the soil. The growth is a sign of shoot and root formation, which is evidence of callus development.

Results

1. How long did it take before callus production began in each plant variety?

2. Which plant variety had the greatest production rate of calluses? What may be the reason for this?

3. Compare your results with known callus production rates for similar plants that are not cloned. Does cloning improve the amount of calluses that form?

4. What important implications does this experiment have for farmers and growers?

7

Sight through Sound I: Can Shape and Color Be Visualized through Sound?

Phase I: Sighted Individuals

Note: This project involves human subjects. For projects involving people, you are required to complete additional forms for the prescreening of your project and approval by a scientific review committee authorized by your state or regional science fair prior to the start of your research.

Purpose

To determine whether colors and shapes can be converted to a melody or a series of tones such that people who hear the sounds can visualize colors and shapes and ultimately a picture.

Hypothesis

Visually impaired persons are said to have a heightened sense of hearing that is attributed to the mind's ability to make up for the lost sense of sight. Therefore, it is hypothesized that a heightened sense of hearing might be used to train the mind of a blind person to convert incoming sounds into images. If images can be converted to sound, then it is hypothesized that visually impaired individuals should be able to "see" by listening.

Materials Needed

- construction paper samples in various colors, such as red, orange, blue, green, yellow, and so on; pictures of various shapes, such as a circle, triangle, square, and diamond

- color chart to help assign various musical notes to colors and shapes
- musical keyboard to play the notes of the colors and shapes
- grid transparency to help map pictures of colors and shapes
- computer to manage project and play back encoded pictures
- 10 sighted volunteers of varying ages and gender
- spreadsheet to tabulate results

Experiment

The first phase of this experiment tests human subjects who are not visually impaired to determine if they can visualize color and shape from hearing various sounds. Initially, tones will be assigned to colors and shapes. The group of sighted individuals will be tested with samples of the colors and shapes. The color and shape samples will be converted into sounds and then played to the sighted audience to determine if they recognize the colors from hearing the melodies. Finally, this group will be tested by hearing a melody for the shapes and then for the colors present in a picture of a simple image containing a variety of these colors and shapes that they have not seen. Their response to this picture will be analyzed to see if they were able to correctly visualize the picture through hearing the melodies associated with the colors and shapes in the picture. Then, in order to rule out sight as a variable related to their being able to visualize shapes and colors from hearing sounds, phase II of this experiment will study visually impaired volunteers who have never seen color. (For this phase of the experiment, see the following project, which was a second-year continuation study.)

Procedure

1. Create a chart of colors and assign a distinct tone to each color, for example:
   > lighter colors = higher pitch
   > darker colors = lower pitch

   Or
   > warmer colors = higher pitch
   > cooler colors = lower pitch

   You can use the following as an example:
   > Yellow = high B
   > Orange = high C sharp
   > Red = D sharp
   > Green = low F
   > Blue = low G

   Then assign another group of notes with a different sound quality to represent the geometric shapes for a circle, a square, a triangle, and a diamond.

2. Create 3 simple pictures with random colors and shapes. With your first picture, place a grid over the picture and identify the prominent color and shape in every square of the grid. Convert each square's color and shape to the assigned tone. Then add an end tone at the end of each row that is drastically different from the tones played for the colors and shapes, for example, 2 very

Yellow		High B	Shape =	
Orange		High C Sharp	○	Low C
Red		D Sharp	□	Low E Flat
Green		Low F	△	Low B Flat
Blue		Low G	◇	Low A Flat

Create a chart of colors and shapes and assign a distinctive musical note to each.

low notes. Record the sequence of tones for each row in the picture and repeat this step for 2 additional pictures.

3. After completing the preparations, gather your group of sighted volunteers and read them these instructions: "I'm performing an experiment where I will play sounds that correspond to different shapes and colors. Once I have played these tones and showed you the colors and shapes they correspond to, I will quiz you on these colors and shapes in random order. After this, I will

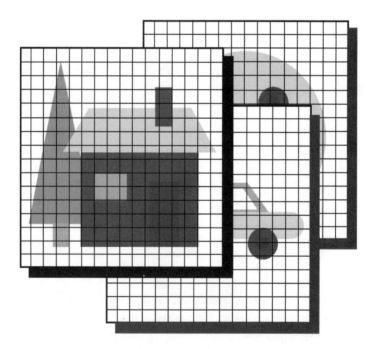

Three pictures of various colors and shapes will be prepared in a grid and converted to various musical notes that will be played for volunteers to see if they can determine the colors and shapes in the pictures by hearing the sounds they have been trained to associate with those colors and shapes.

test you on 3 simple pictures that are made of these colors and shapes. These pictures have been broken down into a grid of notes that are composed of several rows. I will play each row across and at the end of the row you will hear an end tone that sounds different from the rest. This tone indicates the end of a row. Then I will play the following row which will end in the same end tone and then the third row, and so on. After you hear the tones associated with the picture, you will record the colors and shapes that you visualized from the sounds played and will be asked to identify what the picture was."

4. Show the first color to the group of sighted volunteers. Tell them how the color was encoded with sound and how they might recognize the color from hearing the sound. Then ask the volunteers to close their eyes. When their eyes are closed, play the corresponding tone for the first color. Repeat this step for all the other colors.

5. Show the first shape to the group of sighted volunteers. Tell them how the shape was encoded with sound and how they might recognize the shape from hearing the sound. Then ask the volunteers to close their eyes. When their eyes are closed, play the corresponding tone for the first shape. Repeat this step for all the other shapes.

6. Have the volunteers close their eyes again. When their eyes are closed, play the tone of the first color. Ask the volunteers to open their eyes and write down the color that corresponds to the tone they heard. Randomly play tones and have the volunteers record their answers.

7. Have the volunteers close their eyes again. When their eyes are closed, play the tone of the first shape. Ask the volunteers to open their eyes and write down the shape that corresponds to the tone they heard. Randomly play tones and have the volunteers record their answers.

8. Take the first picture that was coded through the grid and play the first line across on the grid followed by the end notes. Ask your volunteers to record the colors and shapes they "heard" in each row. Proceed to the second line of the grid and have them note what they have visualized and continue to the end of the picture. When finished, ask them what they think the composite picture might have been. Repeat for the second two pictures and record all of your data.

Results

1. Were you able to train the volunteers to learn the tones assigned to each color and shape? Did they have difficulty in learning the tones and associating them with the colors and shapes?

2. What was the accuracy of the initial color and shape tone test results for the group? Does this show that the mind can be trained to learn a sound code for color and shape?

3. How did your group perform with the pictures you created? Were they accurate in their visualization of the colors and shapes? Was anyone able to guess what the pictures were?

8

Sight through Sound II: Can Shape and Color Be Visualized through Sound?

Phase II: Visually Impaired Individuals

Note: This project involves human subjects. For projects involving people, you are required to complete additional forms for the prescreening of your project and approval by a scientific review committee authorized by your state or regional science fair prior to the start of your research.

This project is a continuation of a previous year's study. In the first phase of this project, human subjects who are not visually impaired were taught various tones for certain colors and shapes to determine if they can visualize these colors and shapes from hearing the tones (see previous project).

Purpose

To work with actual visually impaired individuals to see if it is possible to teach them how to visualize color and shapes and ultimately a picture even though they have never been able to see what shapes and colors look like.

Materials Needed

- 4 geometric shapes that can be touched, such as wooden blocks in the shape of a circle, triangle, square, and diamond.

- jelly beans in red, yellow, orange, blue, green, yellow, and so on (to aid in the description of color through associating color with a volunteer's sense of taste)

- 3 simple pictures that contain various colors and geometric shapes (from phase I of this project)

- chart to help assign various musical notes to colors and shapes

- musical keyboard to play the notes of the shapes, colors, and pictures
- grid transparency to help map pictures of colors and shapes
- computer to manage project and play back encoded pictures
- 10 visually impaired volunteers of varying ages and gender
- spreadsheet to tabulate results

Experiment

To help explain the experiment conducted in phase I of this project to the visually impaired volunteers, wooden blocks will be used to explain shape and jelly beans will be used to explain color. The jelly beans are to aid in the description of color by associating color with flavor and taste. Once the experiment has been explained, visually impaired volunteers will be tested to see if they can visualize shapes and colors by hearing particular sound tones that are coded for these shapes and colors. Finally, they will be tested to see if they can visualize an actual simple picture.

Procedure

1. Read the following statement to the volunteers: "I'm performing an experiment. In this experiment I am going to play sounds that correspond to different shapes and colors that I will teach to you through your sense of touch and taste. Once I have played these tones and have shown you the colors (flavors) and shapes they correspond to, I will quiz you on these colors and shapes in random order. After this, I will test you on 3 simple pictures that are made of these colors and shapes. These pictures have been encoded in a gridlike fashion. At the end of each row of the grid you will hear a tone that sounds different from the rest. This is the end tone, which represents the end of each row. After 3 pictures, I will quiz you on those pictures in random order. After the final quiz there will be an exam. In the exam there will be some pictures you've never heard. After each picture I will record your answer of the color and shape of the sound."

2. As with the first experiment in phase I of this project, create a chart of colors and assign a distinct tone to each color, for example:

    lighter colors = higher pitch
    darker colors = lower pitch

    Or

    warmer colors = higher pitch
    cooler colors = lower pitch

    You can use the following as an example:

    Yellow = high B
    Orange = high C sharp
    Red = D sharp

			Shape =	
Lemon Flavor	Yellow	High B		
Orange Flavor	Orange	High C Sharp	●	Low C
Cherry Flavor	Red	D Sharp	☐	Low E Flat
Lime Flavor	Green	Low F	▲	Low B Flat
Blueberry or Grape Flavor	Blue	Low G	◆	Low A Flat

Create a chart of colors and shapes and assign a distinctive musical note to each.

Green = low F
Blue = low G

Then assign another group of notes with a different sound quality to represent the geometric shapes of the wooden blocks in the form of a circle, a square, a triangle and a diamond.

3. Assign a particular jelly bean of a certain taste that corresponds to each of the colors you are testing. You can use the following example:

Yellow = lemon flavor
Orange = orange flavor
Red = cherry flavor
Green = lime flavor
Blue = blueberry or grape flavor

4. Give your volunteers the lemon-flavored yellow jelly beans and explain to them that color is to sight as flavor is to taste. Then play the tone for the color yellow. Repeat for each flavor/color until the volunteers recognize and can visualize each color's sound tone.

5. Give your volunteers the first geometric-shaped wooden block and play the tone that corresponds to the shape. Tell them how the shape was encoded with sound and how they might recognize the shape from hearing the sound. Repeat this step for all the other shapes.

6. Once the volunteers are familiar with the colors (flavors) and shapes, and the sounds that are attributed to each color (flavor) and shape, randomly play the tones for colors and shapes and ask the volunteers to record their answers.

7. Take the first picture that has been coded through the grid and play the first line across on the grid followed by the end notes. Ask your volunteers to record the colors and shapes they "heard" in each row. Proceed to the second line of the grid and have them note what they visualized and continue to the end of the picture. When finished, ask them what they think the composite picture might have been. Repeat for the next two pictures and record all of your data.

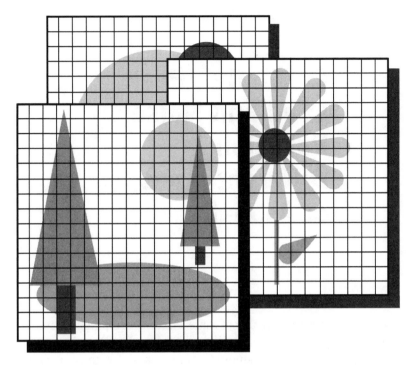

Three pictures of various colors and shapes will be prepared in a grid and converted to various musical notes that will be played for volunteers to see if they can determine the colors and shapes in the pictures by hearing the sounds they have been trained to associate with those colors and shapes.

Results

1. Were you able to train the volunteers to learn the tones assigned to each color through associating color with taste? Were the volunteers able to visualize what the color might look like from knowing what the taste associated with it tasted like? Were you able to train the volunteers to learn the tones assigned to each shape? Did they have difficulty in learning the tones and associating them with the colors and shapes?

2. What was the accuracy of the initial color and shape tone test results for the group? Does this show that the mind can be trained to learn a sound code for color and shape?

3. How did your group perform with the pictures you created? Were they accurate in their visualization of the colors and shapes? Was anyone able to guess what the pictures were?

4. Can visually impaired persons be trained to learn the "language of tones" in order to visualize images?

5. Overall, how do the results obtained from your group of visually impaired volunteers compare with the results obtained from your group of sighted volunteers from the first phase of this project? Does having the gift of sight influence the results of this experiment?

9

Evaluating Peak Load and Noise Pollution in Different Types of Asphalt

Note: This project requires the use of materials and equipment found in an engineering laboratory. The student will need to work with a mentor who is a research engineer or graduate student who can assist with performing certain procedures and operating various types of equipment.

Purpose

First, to determine what sort of pavement is suitable for different environments by evaluating the amount of weight the pavement can withstand under varied conditions. Second, to determine whether noise pollution caused by the contact of automobile tires on road pavement can be reduced by the type of pavement used.

Hypothesis

Noise pollution from highways is a large problem in the United States, especially in residential areas. People who live close to busy roads are subjected to not only the annoyance of noise pollution but also its adverse health effects when sounds exceed a certain decibel level. When a vehicle travels at a speed of 25 miles per hour or greater, most of the noise it creates comes from its tires contacting the road surface. Therefore, it is possible that noise pollution from tire contact may be reduced by the use of different types of road surfaces.

Materials Needed

- 10 different types of commercial asphalt pavement shaped in puck samples (can be obtained from various road paving companies or civil engineering firms)

- Asphalt Pressure Tester with attached computer containing the program Sintech™ (available at some engineering school laboratories)

- oven
- temperature gun
- refrigerator
- acoustical decibel reader
- cotton
- hobby wheel (made of rubber) and axle
- cordless power drill
- water
- vegetable oil

Experiment

The peak load (ITS) that can be withstood by various forms of commercial pavement will be tested using an Asphalt Pressure Tester. Each pavement type will be subjected to different temperatures to see if this change will affect each pavement type's peak load. The noise pollution will be determined by simulating the relationship between the tire and the pavement using a model tire powered by an electric drill to rotate the tire across the pavement. Various environmental conditions will be added to the surfaces of the samples and tested as well to see how each pavement sample performs.

Procedure

Pressure Experiment

1. Place the first sample of asphalt to be tested in the Asphalt Pressure Tester by lifting the brace. Let the pavement sample balance in place before replacing the brace on top.

2. Using the device on the side of the machine, roll the ram so that it is just sitting on top of the brace.

3. Open the Sintech program on the computer beside the testing machine and check to see that it can record data.

4. In the program, a screen will appear that shows the amount of pressure on the pavement before starting the test. This is due to the manual moving of the ram. If the screen shows too much pressure, minimize it by moving the ram up. In an ideal situation, the screen should read 0 lb. of pressure. Click "Run." Testing will begin and an equal amount of pressure will be exerted on the pavement.

5. A graph will appear from the data points received by the computer. Once the pavement sample begins to break apart, the peak pressure will be detailed on the graph and the line will start to move downward. Click "Stop."

6. A chart will then appear with the peak pressure number included.

7. Move the ram up along with the brace and take the sample from the machine. Be careful as the sample could create a mess by breaking apart completely.

8. Repeat steps 1–7 with each pavement type. Accomplishing several trials of the same pavement type is a good way to ensure accurate results.

9. In a large oven, heat several samples of each specimen type to 55°C. Use a temperature gun to point and capture the accurate temperature of each sample. Place each sample at 55°C in the asphalt pressure tester, repeat steps 1–7, and record your data.

10. Repeat steps 1–7 with each asphalt sample heated to 45°C and record your data.

11. Repeat steps 1–7 with each asphalt sample heated to 35°C and record your data.

12. Cool several samples of each pavement type to –20°C. Place each sample at this temperature in the asphalt pressure tester, repeat steps 1–7, and record your data.

13. Repeat steps 1–7 with each asphalt sample cooled to –10°C and record your data.

14. Save all data recorded and graphs for analysis.

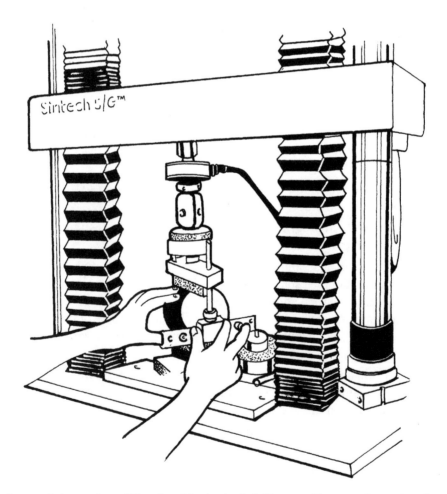

Various asphalt samples will be placed in the Asphalt Pressure Tester to determine the peak load each sample can withstand.

Noise Pollution Experiment

1. On a table, set up the sound decibel reader so that it is at the same height as the road pavement samples being tested. Place it on a platform or even a pile of books if necessary. The sound decibel reader should be set at a rate of 80 and on "slow."

2. Place a layer of cotton under the platform of books the sound decibel reader is resting on and underneath the asphalt sample that will be tested to help eliminate vibration, if necessary.

3. Take the model wheel that is attached to an axle and place it into the head of the drill, winding the top until there is a sturdy connection between the drill and the axle. The tire should rotate on its axle on the drill when the drill is turned on.

4. Place one pavement sample on the cotton in line with the decibel reader.

5. Bring the tire on the drill to the top of the pavement sample and start the drill so that the tire is riding on the pavement sample and steady the drill with your other hand on top. The drill battery should be resting on top of the table so that there is an equal amount of pressure for every test. Wait for the reading to become steady and record the decibel reading of the noise of the tire on the pavement sample.

6. Take 10 trials of each pavement type to ensure accurate results.

7. Repeat steps 4–6 for each pavement type.

8. Soak the various road pavement samples in a large bucket of water for 12 hours. This is to simulate what pavement would be like on a rainy day.

9. After 12 hours, take the samples out of the water and repeat steps 4–6 on each of the samples. When spinning the tire on the pavement, it can dry the water on the surface; therefore, for accurate results, rotate the pavement slightly for continuous water on the surface.

10. After the pavement samples are completely dry, place a layer of vegetable oil on top of every pavement sample. This is to simulate an extremely hot day when oil starts to form at the surface of pavement. Repeat steps 4–6 with all the road pavement samples.

11. Place the different types of road pavement in a freezer with a temperature of −10°C. This is to simulate what pavement would be like on a cold day.

12. Once the samples reach −10°C, repeat steps 4–6 on every sample.

    Save all decibel readings recorded for analysis.

Results

1. Analyze your results from the pressure part of the experiment. What sample was the strongest with highest peak pressure? What sample was the strongest with highest peak pressure under different temperatures?

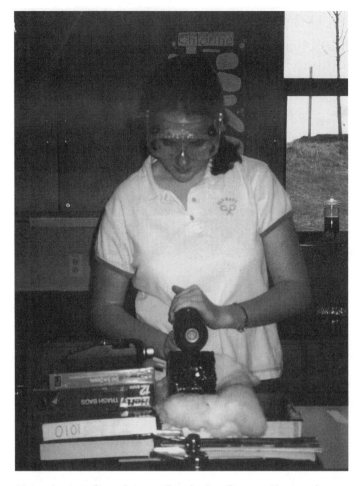

Massachusetts State Science Fair finalist Gemma Kite performing the noise pollution part of her experiment.

2. Which sample created the most noise? Which created the least? Which sample created the most noise under the various simulated weather conditions? The least?

3. What may account for the amount of noise caused by a pavement sample?

4. What types of payment proved to be best for hot or dry conditions? For a relatively cool climate?

5. Is there any correlation between pavement strength and amount of noise pollution?

10

Effects of Garlic and Vitamin C on High Blood Pressure in Human Subjects

Note: This project involves human subjects. For projects involving people, you are required to complete additional forms for the prescreening of your project and approval by a scientific review committee authorized by your state or regional science fair prior to the start of your research.

Purpose

To determine the effects of garlic and vitamin C, both individually and in combination, on mean systolic and diastolic blood pressure in human subjects with mild hypertension.

Hypothesis

Prevention and treatment of high blood pressure are critical to reducing the incidence of heart attacks and strokes. Lifestyle modifications have been known to be one of the most important tools for effective control of blood pressure. Many studies have shown that the intake of minerals, such as potassium and calcium, and a low intake of sodium should be the focus of dietary modification. However, antioxidants, such as garlic and vitamin C, which are said to be beneficial in treating a number of health ailments, may also have an effect on blood pressure.

Materials Needed

- 12 volunteers with medically diagnosed mild hypertension (You will need to work with a medical doctor who can act as a mentor to you to obtain access to the volunteers and administer the supplements to them. Ask your family doctor or call your local hospital to make contact with a physician who treats hypertension.)

- garlic tablets containing 1,250 mg garlic per tablet
- vitamin C tablets containing 500 mg of ascorbic acid in each tablet
- digital blood pressure machine for systolic and diastolic blood pressure (mmHg) monitoring
- Computer with Microsoft Word, graphics, and statistical software

Experiment

The effects of garlic and vitamin C supplements in 12 human subjects with mild hypertension will be followed for a period of one month. Four volunteers will be given a 30-day supply of garlic tablets and instructions for taking the supplement daily. Four volunteers will be given a 30-day supply of vitamin C and instructions for taking the supplement daily. Four volunteers will be given a 30-day supply of both tablets and instructions for taking them daily. Once the volunteers have begun taking the supplements, each volunteer will have his or her blood pressure measured at the end of each week for a period of 4 consecutive weeks while taking the supplements. The average resting systolic and diastolic blood pressure will be measured for each person and recorded.

Procedure

1. Through your physician identify 12 patients with mild hypertension who would be willing to volunteer their time for one month to participate in your study. Your physician should also confirm that the volunteers are not allergic to the supplements and will not experience any adverse drug interaction with the supplements.

2. Divide the group into 3 sets. One set will be given the vitamin C supplements, one will be given the garlic supplements, and another will be given a combination of both.

3. Create a progress chart for each patient and note his or her name, age, weight, height, sex, and blood pressure at the start of the 30-day period.

4. Arrange a time and place with your physician for you to explain the experiment and have the physician administer the pills to the volunteers. Read the following statement to the group: "I am conducting an experiment to see if garlic supplements, vitamin C supplements, or a combination of both have any effect in reducing your blood pressure. The first group will be asked to take one garlic pill supplement every day at lunchtime for a period of 30 days, the second group will be asked to take one vitamin C pill every day at lunchtime for a period of 30 days, and the third group will be asked to take both one garlic pill and one vitamin C pill every day at lunchtime for 30 days. You will be given a calendar chart to place on your refrigerator to serve as a reminder to take the pills. You will be asked to check off every day you took your pills and note how you felt for the day. I then will arrange a time and place where I can take your blood pressure at the end of each week for a period of 4 weeks. Thank you for your participation in this study. I will start

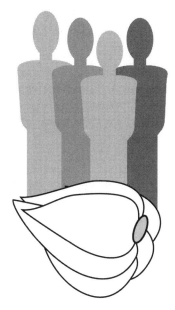

Four volunteers will be given garlic supplements for 30 days.

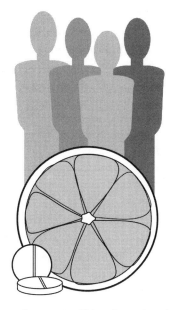

Four volunteers will be given vitamin C supplements for 30 days.

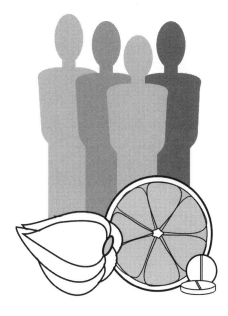

Four volunteers will be given a combination of garlic and vitamin C supplements for 30 days.

the experiment today and will take your blood pressure right now." Then record the systolic and diastolic blood pressure readings for each volunteer and pass out the supplements and calendar charts to the volunteers.

5. Be sure to make arrangements at the outset of the experiment to set a convenient time and place where you can take the volunteers' blood pressure weekly. This might be at the physician's office (if he or she can set aside the time) or you might be able to visit each volunteer at his or her home to take a blood pressure reading. When taking a volunteer's blood pressure you will be recording both systolic and diastolic readings.

6. At the end of the month gather the calendar chart information from each volunteer along with his or her blood pressure readings for the 30-day period and analyze your results.

Results

1. What were the systolic and diastolic blood pressure readings for the group at the outset of the experiment? What were their weekly readings? What were the readings at the conclusion of the 30-day period?

2. Was there any change in the blood pressure readings for the group who took just the vitamin C? Was there any change in the blood pressure readings for the group who took just the garlic? What about the group who took a combination of both?

3. If there were any changes, did these changes occur in both systolic and diastolic blood pressure or both?

4. What group, if any, experienced the most positive results? Did any group experience negative results? Did the combination of vitamin C and garlic create a more positive result among that group of volunteers given both supplements?

11

The Chladni Effect: Is There a Relationship between the Frequencies Produced and Patterns Created Using Bowed Plates of Various Metals?

Purpose

To determine whether there is a relationship between the frequencies produced and the patterns created using bowed plates of various metals.

Hypothesis

In the late eighteenth century the German physicist Ernst E. F. Chladni, often called the father of acoustics, conducted studies with fixed plates that were set to vibrate at various frequencies with the use of a violin bow. Chladni found that when fine sand was sprinkled across the plates in vibration, various nodal lines and patterns were exhibited under different frequencies. All objects have a set of natural frequencies at which they vibrate, and each frequency is associated with a standing wave pattern. There may be a relationship between the frequency produced and the sand patterns created on the vibrating plates.

Materials Needed

- metal clamp fastened to the end of a workbench (to hold plates in place)
- various metal plates, namely polycarbonate, carbon steel, aluminum, stainless steel, copper, and so on, that are approx. 1.5–1.6 mm in thickness and approx. 30 x 30 cm in size
- violin bow and rosin
- cup of sand
- digital multimeter capable of measuring frequency connected to a microphone and radio receiver/amplifier
- camera to photograph sand patterns at different frequencies, or paper to sketch patterns

Experiment

Various metal plates will be fixed into position in the metal clamp. Sand will be strewn across the top of each metal plate and a violin bow will be dragged across various edges of the metal plate to create various vibrations. The frequencies of these vibrations will be recorded. At the same time, various nodal lines and patterns of sand created by the different frequencies of vibration will be photographed or drawn and recorded.

Procedure

1. Find a workbench with a metal clamp in which to mount the various metal plates that will be tested. If you cannot find a workbench with a clamp or do not have someone to mount one for you, you can improvise by drilling a hole in a workbench or work table. Insert a bolt up through the hole and use a metal pipe as a spacer. Put a metal washer on top of the pipe. Put a metal plate on top of the washer, and put a nut on top to hold it down.

2. Find a means to measure the frequencies produced by the plates that are being vibrated. A digital multimeter capable of measuring frequency and connected to a microphone may work alone if the microphone is close enough to the plate. However, if no vibrations are noticeably measured with these instruments, you might need to connect a radio receiver/amplifier between the microphone and the meter. Set the meter to frequency (Hz) and place it next to the microphone.

3. Take one plate and mark 24 regions on the plate. Give each region a number. Each of these regions will be bowed with the violin bow. Secure the plate to the metal clamp (or whatever device you developed to hold the plate in place) and activate your meter and amplifier.

4. Rosin the violin bow and sprinkle some sand (about a tablespoon) evenly onto the plate.

5. Bow each region of the plate that is marked with the violin bow, record all stable frequencies, and photograph or sketch each sand pattern that occurs for each stable frequency. Record your data.

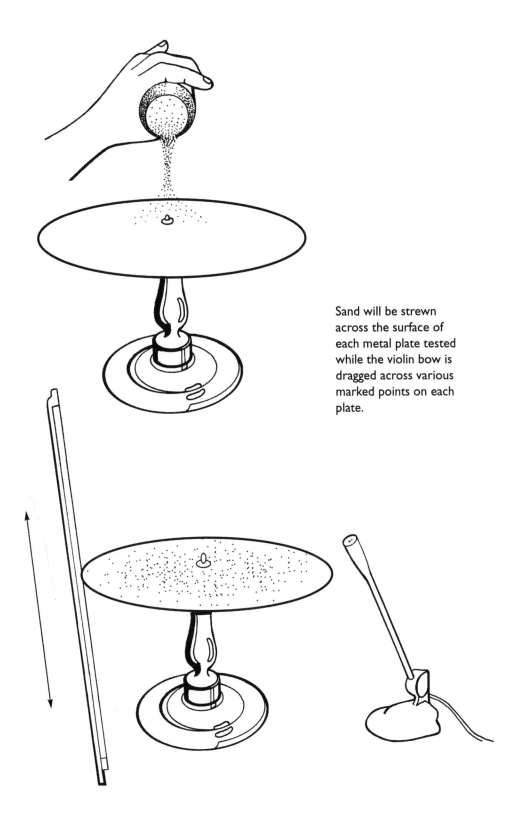

Sand will be strewn across the surface of each metal plate tested while the violin bow is dragged across various marked points on each plate.

6. Repeat steps 3–5 for each plate. Carefully log all frequencies for each region on each plate and the corresponding sand pattern that was created by each.

Various sand patterns you might see for different frequencies achieved when the bow is dragged along a plate.

Results

1. On each plate, what were the frequencies in each of the 24 regions that were bowed? Did they differ?

2. On each plate, what were the sand patterns for each of the 24 regions that were bowed? Did they differ?

3. Did different plates yield the same frequencies when bowed in the same regions? Did different plates yield the same sand patterns when bowed in the same regions? Did different plates yield the same patterns at the same frequencies?

4. Were more complex patterns produced at higher frequencies?

12

Natural Attic Ventilation

Note: The following project illustrates how an engineering project differs from a conventional science fair project. An engineering project involves designing, building, troubleshooting, or demonstrating a working model of a new product, a device to improve upon an existing model or product, or an inventive model or device that addresses or solves an existing problem. In this particular project example, prior knowledge and skill in carpentry and building, or the assistance of a mentor with experience in this area, is required.

Purpose

To engineer an attic ventilation system in which the air will be exchanged from the attic more often, thereby providing a cooler home and possibly reducing the air conditioning needs of the homeowner. The efficiency of this design will then be compared with a standard design for ventilating an attic.

Hypothesis

A conventional attic contains a standard ventilation system. The attic gets hot in the summer due to the lack of air flow. The air sits in the attic and is heated by the radiant energy on the roof. This type of design has only one air exchange per minute. Thus, it might be possible for a ventilation system to be designed to cool attic air naturally by increasing its air exchanges per minute.

Materials Needed

- 7 twelve-feet long 2 x 8 spruce planks
- 15 eight-feet long 2 x 4 spruce studs
- 5 8 x 4 feet sheets of ½-inch thick chipboard
- 4 boxes of common nails
- 1 bag of R19 insulation
- 3 boxes of roofing nails
- drywall sheets
- 1 roll of tar paper
- 2 soffit vents
- 1 conventional ridge vent
- 2 eight-feet-long 2 x 3 spruce studs
- 1 1x3 spruce stud
- 1 roll of common fly screen (used for window screens)
- 1 box of staples
- 2 cans of Great Stuff liquid foam

Tools Needed

- measuring tape
- hammer
- wide-tooth saw
- fine-tooth saw
- electric saw
- square
- level
- drill
- utility knife
- staple gun
- digital thermometer

Experiment

Two miniature houses, each 63x65x40 inches (about the size of a dog house), will be built in exactly the same manner and studied. One will have a standard ventilation system, which is designed to have only one air exchange per minute, and the other will have a custom ventilation system that is engineered to have several air exchanges per minute. Once it has been constructed, temperatures at various times during the warmer summer months will be recorded to see which house stays the coolest.

Procedure

Phase I: Construct the Houses

1. The houses should be built and framed with the materials listed above. If you do not have carpentry experience, ask an adult who does to help you. The design of the houses should be basic; the following general guidelines will help you construct the houses for testing.

2. Start by making frames for the base of the house using the 2 x 8s. Then make the wall frames using the 2 x 4s.

3. Cut the chipboard to size and nail it to the base of the house, forming the floor. Nail the wall frames to the base and connect the chipboard to the wall frames.

4. Place R19 insulation in between the wall frame studs.

5. Drill a small hole through the center of a wall through which a thermometer will be inserted into the house to measure the room temperature.

6. Nail drywall to the inside walls.

7. Use the 2 x 8s to frame the rafters. Nail drywall to separate the bottom room from the attic. Put the rafter frame on top of the bottom room. Nail chipboard to the rafters to form the roof.

8. Cover the roof with tar paper to protect the chipboard from precipitation.

9. The important difference between the two houses is the attic ventilation systems. The ventilation systems in both houses have a soffit vent where the air enters the attic, but they will each have a different type of ridge vent where

Delaware Valley Regional Science Fair award winner Paul Boland constructing the test homes.

the air exits the attic. The standard house has a 1 x 34-inch opening between the main beam and the chipboard roof. However, on the standard ventilation house this opening will be covered with the conventional ridge vent. The custom ventilation house has a 2 x 34-inch opening between the chipboard and each side of the main beam. This opening will be covered with the custom-engineered ridge vent that will be constructed in the next step.

10. To construct the custom ridge vent, cut 2 x 3s into 6 blocks each 12 inches long. Take these blocks and cut an angle on one side of each. This angle will have a 4-inch rise per 12 inches. The end of the 2 x 3 with this angle is the end that sits on top of the roof (the rafters have a 4-inch rise per 12 inches). A sharper angle will need to be made on the other ends of the 2 x 3s. This sharper angle has a 2-inch rise for every 2½ inches. Nail the sharper ends of these 2 x 3s to a 1 x 3 stud, three on each side of the 1 x 3 with a space of 16 inches between every 2 x 3. Staple the common fly screen to the 2 x 3 frame. (This is to protect the inside of the attic from animal entry.) Then, nail this frame of six 2 x 3s to the rafters of the custom made house.

11. Cut the chipboard to two sections of 38 x 9 inches, and nail these two sections to the tops of the 2 x 3 frame to form a roof. Then staple one piece of tar paper over this roof. Then cut 2 pieces of chipboard to 6 x 10 inches, with the top of these pieces cut with an angle to match the angles on the 2 x 3s. These pieces will be nailed to the ends of the frame.

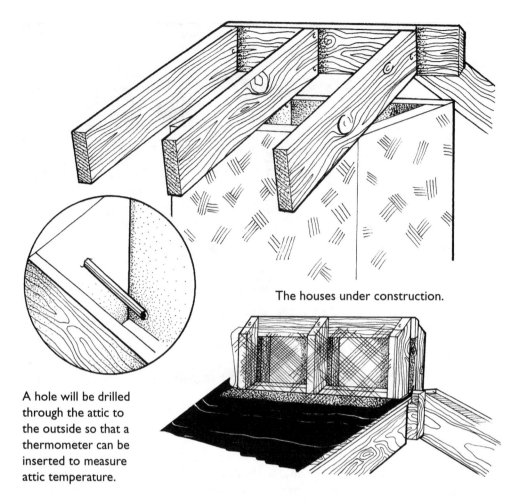

The houses under construction.

A hole will be drilled through the attic to the outside so that a thermometer can be inserted to measure attic temperature.

12. For the standard soffit vent, make a hole between the ends of the rafters and the wall of the house (this is where a soffit vent normally goes). The hole should be 10 x 32 inches. Cover the hole with a standard soffit vent. For the custom soffit vent, make a 13 x 36-inch hole between the ends of the rafters and the wall of the house. Then cover the hole with common fly screen for the soffit vent.

13. Cover the sides of the attic with pieces of chipboard. Then drill a hole into the attic to the outside of both houses so that the attic temperature can be measured.

14. If there are any small openings or gaps in the houses you built, you can fill in these areas with any type of filling product. However, in this project, Great Stuff brand was used to fill in the little holes in both houses.

Phase II: Test the Houses

1. Calculate how many air exchanges the attics had per minute by using the standard airflow due to wind velocity formula. This formula can be found in books about physics or engineering.

2. Using a precise temperature digital thermometer, take the temperatures in the houses. Record the temperatures in the attic and bottom room in the standard ventilation house morning, noon, and night. At the same time, record the outside temperature. Repeat this procedure for the custom ventilation house. Continue this procedure for 2 months, preferably during warmer months.

3. After you obtain your results, average the temperatures for each house per week. Examine the difference (if any) in temperature between the two attics and statistically determine the percentage by which the custom ventilation system is more effective at keeping the house cooler than the standard system.

Results

1. What was the air exchange per minute for each house?

2. How did the temperatures between the two houses compare during the 2-month period? Which house proved to be cooler on average?

3. Did one system perform better than the other overall? Did one system perform better than the other at various times of the day?

4. Were there any problems with the custom ventilation system that had an effect on its operation? What else could be done to improve the custom attic ventilation design?

13

Legal Tender or Criminal Evidence?

An International Science and Engineering Fair Project

Note: This project involves testing for a controlled substance, and therefore you are required to work with an authorized forensic scientist under strict guidelines and complete additional forms for the prescreening of your project and approval by a scientific review committee authorized by your state or regional science fair prior to the start of your research. Additionally, this project requires the use of materials and equipment found in a forensic chemistry laboratory.

Purpose

To determine if traces of cocaine residue are present on a random sampling of currency acquired from a local financial institution.

Hypothesis

Statistics indicate that cocaine use has increased in recent years. The drug is often taken by inhaling the powdery substance into the nose through a straw or rolled up currency. Studies by the Federal Bureau of Investigation and recent national news reports have indicated that a large percentage of currency in circulation today contains traces of cocaine. Testing a random sampling of currency may uncover traces of this drug and may indicate usage of the drug in a particular geographic location.

Materials Needed

- ten $1, $5, $10, $20, $50, and $100 bills with recent issue date
- sterile latex gloves
- apron
- safety goggles
- 60 50-ml test tubes
- labeling stickers
- 1,000 ml methanol
- beaker
- 2 pairs of tweezers

- 60 rubber stoppers for test tubes
- test tube racks
- paper towels
- fume hood
- one 10-microliter syringe
- gas chromatograph mass spectrometer

Experiment

Sixty bills, 10 each in the denominations of $1, $5, $10, $20, $50, and $100, will be obtained from the same source (local financial institution) and will all have a recent issue date (to ensure that any traces of cocaine found are from recent usage). The bills will be washed in test tubes containing methanol to remove any residue from the bills. Once the samples have been washed and the methanol has been allowed to evaporate from the tube, the remaining residue will be tested with the use of a gas chromatograph mass spectrometer for the purpose of identifying traces of cocaine on the currency.

Procedure

1. Put on the apron, latex gloves, and safety goggles.
2. Place a labeling sticker with a sample number on each test tube and stopper. Each tube should be labeled with an increasing number, using the bill denomination as the first number and the sample number as the second identifier. Record the corresponding sample number next to the appropriate bill serial number in a log book.
3. Measure 30 milliliters of methanol into a beaker and pour into one test tube.
4. Roll one bill sample into a cylindrical shape.
5. Submerge the bill into the test tube using a pair of tweezers.
6. Securely place a stopper on the test tube.
7. Shake the test tube for approximately one minute.
8. Place the test tube in the test tube rack.
9. Remove stopper from the test tube.

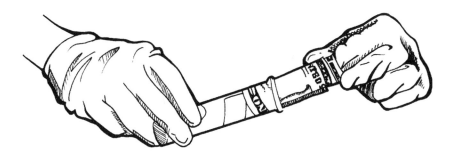

Roll one sample bill into a cylinder and place it into a test tube containing methanol with the tweezers or sterile gloves.

Place a stopper on the test tube and shake for one minute.

10. Using both pairs of tweezers, carefully remove the bill. Hold the bill directly above the test tube and gently squeeze with the tweezers to allow more of the methanol to drip back into the test tube.

11. Unroll the bill and lay it flat on a paper towel to dry.

12. Repeat steps 3–11 for each bill to be sampled.

13. Leave all test tubes uncovered under the fume hood and allow the methanol to evaporate to approximately 1–2 milliliters of solution. Be sure to monitor the samples regularly to check the evaporation progress.

14. Once samples have evaporated sufficiently, use a 10-microliter syringe to inject approximately 1 microliter of solution from a sample into the gas chromatograph mass spectrometer. Rinse the syringe with methanol to clean it.

Using both pairs of tweezers, carefully remove the sample bill
from the test tube by holding it directly above the tube.
Squeeze any absorbed methanol from the bill into the tube.

15. The gas chromatograph separates the compounds and then sends the separated compounds to the mass spectrometer, where they are identified by mass.

16. A computer program will identify the molecular weight and search for the three molecular weights that combine to form cocaine, namely, 82, 182, and 303.

17. Analyze each reading to see if the 3 molecular weights appear simultaneously, thereby providing positive evidence of cocaine.

18. Repeat steps 14–17 for each bill sample and record your data results.

Results

1. Did any of the bills test positive for traces of cocaine? What percentage of the bills, if any, contained traces of cocaine?

2. Did lower or higher denominations of bills studied have a higher percentage of cocaine residue?

3. What factors—such as the source of the currency sampled, the denomination of the bills sampled, and the length of time the currency has been in circulation—might affect the end results of this study?

Chelsea Grigery with her project at the Intel ISEF.

14

Can Mosquitoes Be Safely and Effectively Eliminated through Identifying the Variables That Attract Them?

Purpose

To determine a safer way to repel mosquitoes by identifying various factors that attract a mosquito so that these variables may be isolated and used to lure mosquitoes to a remote area and effectively keep them away from people without the use of harmful chemical repellents or pesticides.

Hypothesis

Mosquitoes have always been considered pests. However, in recent years they have come to pose a serious health risk as some members of this species have been linked to West Nile virus, a sometimes fatal disease. For many years, the best defense against mosquitoes was deet, a chemical insect repellent that is sprayed on the skin. However, this repellent as well as other chemical pesticides, has been linked to adverse health problems and the contamination of soil, food, water, and air. Therefore, a safer way to eliminate mosquitoes might be to find out what attracts mosquitoes and create lures out of that material to lead the mosquitoes away from humans.

Materials Needed

Note: Be sure to dress in pants and long sleeves while conducting the experiment to protect yourself against an unwanted mosquito bite.

- Area with a mosquito population (such as a backyard or park near a pond or swamp in warm weather, if available; otherwise a small wading pool filled with water can be used)
- 6 buckets
- tap water
- thermometer
- plastic wrap and tape
- Fly paper or other adhesive material for trapping flying insects
- empty shoeboxes or facial tissues lined with colored construction paper
- 3 large bowls
- package of raw hamburger meat
- sweetened soft drink
- paper towels
- spray perfume
- gloves
- block of dry ice approximately 3x2x1 inches in size

Experiment

Since it is widely known that mosquitoes tend to breed near stagnant water, the experiment will be conducted in a backyard or park near a pond or swamp. If a natural water source is unavailable, a small pool of water, such as a child's wading pool, can be set up in a backyard. Sheets of flypaper will be set alongside each variable being tested to observe the number of mosquitoes trapped, if any. Several variables will be tested separately and apart from each other to determine which factor may lure the most mosquitoes—smell, temperature, color, or carbon dioxide.

Procedure

1. *Test for the temperature as a variable.* Fill four buckets fully with water of varying temperatures that you should measure with your thermometer—hot (approx. 140°F), warm (approx. 95°F), cool (approx. 60°F), and cold (approx. 40°F). Place plastic wrap around the top of each bucket and seal with tape so

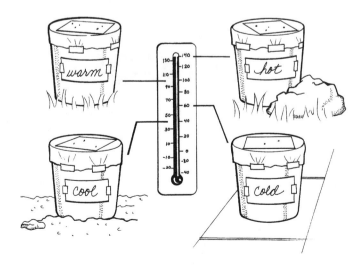

Test for temperature as a variable.

that the buckets do not release any moisture. Secure one sheet of flypaper on top of each container. Place the buckets at various points in the yard or park away from one another. Observe the activity on each bucket for an hour. After the hour is up, note the number of mosquitoes trapped by the flypaper and record your results.

2. *Test for color as a variable.* Line the inside and outside panels of the bottoms of several empty shoe boxes or facial tissue boxes with a different color construction paper. Be sure to use colors of various tones and hues. Secure the flypaper either inside or alongside each box. Distribute the boxes at various points in the yard or park away from one another. Observe the activity on each colored box for an hour. After the hour is up, note the number of mosquitoes trapped by the flypaper and record your results.

3. *Test for smell as a variable.* Place the hamburger meat in a bowl, the soda in another bowl, and spray the perfume onto paper towels and place the towels in another bowl. Secure flypaper on or around each bowl. Distribute the bowls at various points away from each other in the yard or park. Observe the activity around each bowl for an hour. After the hour is up, note the number of mosquitoes trapped by the flypaper and record your results.

4. *Test for carbon dioxide as a variable.* Line the bottoms of two buckets with flypaper. Put on the gloves and place the block of dry ice (a solid form of carbon dioxide) in one of the buckets. Distribute the buckets at various points away from each other in the yard or park. Observe the activity in each bucket for an hour. After the hour is up, note the number of mosquitoes trapped by the flypaper and record your results.

5. Repeat steps 1–4 in two different locations to ensure that data is consistent and reliable.

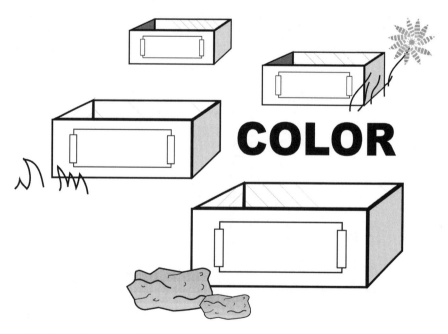

Test for color as a variable.

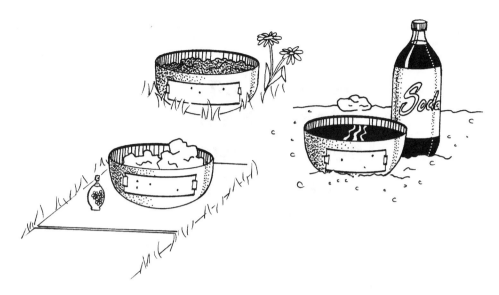

Test for smell as a variable.

Results

1. Which water temperature, if any, seemed to attract the most mosquitoes? What color, if any, seemed to attract the most mosquitoes? What smell seemed to attract the most mosquitoes? Did the carbon dioxide emitted from the block of dry ice attract mosquitoes?

2. Were the results consistent for each location tested?

3. Which variable seemed to attract the most mosquitoes overall?

4. Based on the results of the experiment, what type of device could be effectively constructed to lure and trap mosquitoes and effectively keep them away from living areas?

15

Does Coating Metals Prevent Their Corrosion? A Study of the Effect of Corrosion on Metals in Different Environments

Purpose

To determine how different types of metals corrode in specific environments and whether coating or painting metals with epoxy paint or primer will slow down or prevent the corrosion process.

Hypothesis

A big concern for various buildings, bridges, cars, tools, pipes, as well as anything else made of metal, is the prevention of corrosion. Corrosion causes the breakdown of metal and compromises its use and safety. Corrosion is typically brought on from exposure to chemicals and environmental factors. Not all metals seem to corrode in the same way or at the same rate. Additionally, treating metals with epoxy paint or primer might retard or prevent the corrosion of certain metals.

Materials Needed

- 32 containers (large enough to hold one piece or sheet of metal and liquid)
- 8 pieces/small sheets of carbon steel
- 8 pieces/small sheets of stainless steel
- 8 pieces/small sheets of aluminum

- 8 pieces/small sheets of copper
- tap water
- seawater (or saltwater)
- calcium chloride solution
- 3 empty spray bottles
- epoxy paint or primer for metals
- paint brushes

Experiment

Various metals will be placed in different water solutions—saltwater, calcium chloride, and tap water. All will be placed outside for 15 days. After 15 days, the specimens will be removed from the solutions and left outdoors. They will be sprayed every other day with their same water-type solutions for a period of 15 days and observed. Then epoxy paint or primer will be painted on the same types of metals, and they will be tested in the same way to see if these coatings will retard or prevent the corrosion of these metals when placed in each of the water solutions.

Procedure

1. Place one piece or sheet of carbon steel in a container filled with tap water. Make sure that the metal is completely submersed in the tap water. Do the same with the stainless steel, the aluminum, and the copper, each in a separate container filled with tap water. Mark each container for metal and liquid type. Take the containers outdoors and leave for 15 days. Check the metals every other day. At the end of the 15 days, examine the metals fully and note the amounts of corrosion or surface changes, if any, on each specimen.

2. Repeat step 1 with the seawater, the calcium chloride solution, and the empty containers (the metal in the empty containers will be your control).

3. At the end of the 15 days, take the metal pieces out of their containers, being careful to keep them separate and identifiable, and place the metals on a driveway, patio, or picnic table. Spray the metals every other day for 15 days with the same solution that each specimen metal was submersed in previously. Observe and record results during and at the end of the 15-day period.

4. Take the remaining pieces of each metal type and paint them with the epoxy primer or paint. Make sure each piece is evenly coated and that all pieces are covered equally. Repeat steps 1–3 and record your results.

Results

1. Did any of the metals corrode? If so, which type corroded the most in all environments? Which corroded the least? What may account for these results?

2. Which environment produced the most corrosion, if any? What may account for this result?

3. Was corrosion absent or the rate of corrosion slower in the metals coated with the epoxy primer or paint?

4. What practical applications might this experiment have for the construction of buildings, bridges, or other metal structures or devices left outdoors in various environments?

16

Are Rodents Territorial?

Note: Check with your teacher or science fair adviser for appropriate forms and permission to work on this project because strict rules apply to experiments involving vertebrate animals. You are required to complete additional forms for the prescreening of your project and approval by a scientific review committee authorized by your state or regional science fair prior to starting your research.

Purpose

To determine if mice and rats become aggressive when another mouse or rat is introduced into their space and if there are other factors that influence this behavior.

Hypothesis

Mice and rats are often considered social, gentle animals that make great pets. However, mice and rats may become territorial when another mouse or rat intrudes on their space and may act aggressively or defensivly. If territoriality does exist, there may be other factors that influence this behavior, such as gender, age, pregnancy, or the onset of heat.

Materials Needed

- 3 male mice: one 6 months, one 12 months, and one 18 months old. 3 female mice: one 6 months, one 12 months, and one 18 months old. One female mouse should be pregnant or in heat. 3 male rats: one 6 months, one 12 months, and one 18 months old. 3 female rats: one 6 months, one 12 months, and one 18 months old. One female rat should be pregnant or in heat.
- 12 cages in which to keep the mice and rats

- bedding for cages, such as soft paper, wood chips, or shavings. The material should be absorbent and changed twice per week.

- food for the mice and rats, such as grains and meat products, fruit, or commercially available rodent pellets, which are easy to use and provide a reliable diet

- water feeders with fresh water for each cage

Experiment

The 6 mice will be placed in their respective cages and be allowed to establish their own territory or home on their own for about a month. Once the mice have settled into their homes, they will be tested to see if any variables, such as sex, age, pregnancy, or the onset of mating season (heat), cause territoriality in a mouse when an intruder is allowed entry into a mouse's home. This experiment will be repeated with the rats. Observations will be made among each group to determine which variable, if any, creates territorialism. Then the mice and rats will be compared to one another to see if they exhibit similar behaviors.

Procedure

1. Set up a separate home for each mouse with bedding, food, and fresh water. Be sure to clean the cages and bedding of the residents at least twice per week and ensure a daily fresh supply of food and water. Allow each mouse about 30 days to get comfortable and settled into its home.

2. Test the sex variable as a factor.

   a. Allow a female mouse (FM1 = female mouse 1) that is not pregnant or in heat to be admitted into the home of one of the male mice (MM1 = male mouse 1). As soon as she enters the male's home, observe the male's behavior carefully. Note any aggressiveness, hoarding of food, or other behavior changes in the male mouse. (Be sure to remove the female mouse quickly from the cage if she is danger of being harmed by the male mouse or vice versa.) Try to keep the female in the cage with the male mouse for an hour (if possible) and closely observe the male's behavior, making detailed notes throughout the hour. At the end of the hour, return the female to her cage and allow both mice to get comfortable again in their own homes.

   b. Take a different male mouse (MM2) and allow him entrance into the home of a different female mouse (FM2) that is not pregnant or in heat and perform the same evaluation. Try to keep the male in the cage with the female mouse for an hour (if possible) and closely observe the female's behavior, making detailed notes throughout the hour. (Remember to remove the male mouse quickly from the cage if he is in danger of being harmed by the female mouse or vice versa.)

   c. When all the mice have adjusted comfortably back in their homes, take MM1 and allow him entry into the home of the third male mouse (MM3) and perform the same evaluation. Try to keep MM1 in the cage with MM3 for an hour (if possible) and closely observe MM3's behavior, making detailed notes throughout the hour. (Remember to remove MM1 quickly from the cage if he is in danger of being harmed by MM3, or vice versa.)

   d. Take FM2 and allow her entry into the home of FM1 and perform the same evaluation. Try to keep FM2 in the cage with FM1 for an hour (if possible) and closely observe FM1's behavior, making detailed notes

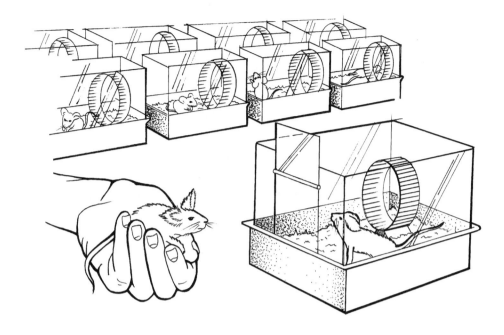

Once the rodents have independently adapted to their homes for 30 days they will be introduced to each other under certain conditions to determine the presence of territoriality.

throughout the hour. (Remember to remove FM2 quickly from the cage if she is in danger of being harmed by the FM1, or vice versa.)

e. *Note:* Leave FM3, which is pregnant or in heat, or has a litter, out of this experiment.

3. Test the age variable as a factor. Perform the same type of intrusion test, this time introducing each male into the other male mouse homes to note the behavioral changes of each male when a different aged male is introduced into the home. Perform the same test with both FM1 and FM2. Again, leave FM3 out of this experiment.

4. Test the variable of pregnancy or heat.

a. Take any male mouse and allow him entry into the home of FM3. As soon as he enters the female's home observe the female's behavior carefully. Note any aggressiveness, nervousness, hoarding of food, mating behavior, or other behavior changes in the female mouse. (Be sure to remove the male mouse quickly from the cage if he is danger of being harmed by the female mouse or vice versa.) Try to keep the male in the cage with the female mouse for an hour (if possible) and closely observe the female's behavior, making detailed notes throughout the hour. At the end of the hour, return the male to his cage and allow both mice to get comfortable again in their own homes.

5. Repeat steps 1-4 with the rats. Be careful to note the identity of each rat—male rat 1 (MR1), female rat 1 (FR1), on so on. Make detailed notes of each intrusion.

Results

1. Did any of the mice become territorial when it encountered the intruder? If so, under which variables did you observe territorial behavior?

2. Did any of the rats become territorial when it met the intruder? If so, under which variables did you observe territorial behavior.

3. If territorial behavior was detected, what type of territorial behavior did the male mice exhibit when intruded upon? What type of territorial behavior did the female mice exhibit when intruded upon?

4. If territorial behavior was detected, what type of territorial behavior did the male rats exhibit when intruded upon? What type of territorial behavior did the female rats exhibit when intruded upon?

5. Were the mice or the rats more territorial? Was any group docile or social when an intruder was introduced?

17

Can Water Hardness Be Determined through Soap Bubbles?

Purpose

To see if it is possible to estimate the hardness of a variety of waters from various wells and public water supply sources solely by their bubble activity after being mixed with soap and shaken.

Hypothesis

Hard water has a high dissolved mineral content of calcium, magnesium, and other minerals. Water hardness is often expressed in grains per gallon (gpg), milligrams per liter (mg/l) or parts per million (ppm). One grain of hardness equals 17.1 mg/l. Water is considered hard when it contains between 7-10.5 gpg or 120-180 mg/l of these minerals. Hard water is generally not considered a health risk but it is not desirable to have hard water because the minerals can build up on pipes and leave film and stains around sinks and tubs, and hard water tends to not mix well with detergents. Therefore, since it is known that hard water does not mix well with soaps or detergents, it should be possible to estimate the hardness of water by testing how many bubbles are produced when a mixture of a water sample and soap is shaken.

Materials Needed

- 5 1-liter containers
- 5 liters distilled water
- calcium chloride (magnesium chloride can be substituted)
- test tubes (one for each benchmark solution and one for each water sample tested)
- pipettes
- liquid hand soap
- stoppers for the test tubes
- black marking pen
- test tube racks

- tap water from various locations that include either a well or a public water supply

- hard water test kit (drop titration kit)

Experiment

Various benchmark solutions of hard and soft water containing specific amounts of calcium chloride added to distilled water (to imitate soft water, slightly hard water, moderately hard water, hard water, and very hard water) will be prepared, added to test tubes with a drop of liquid hand soap, and then tested for the amount of soap bubbles they produce when shaken. Then actual samples of tap water from wells and various public water supply sources will be tested with the liquid hand soap to see how many bubbles they each produce. The results will then be compared with the results from the bench-mark solutions and a guess or estimate will be made as to how hard the actual water samples are. Finally, each sample will be tested with a hard water test kit to measure the actual amount of minerals present in each sample. These results will be compared to the hardness estimates to see if soap bubble formation is a reliable indicator of water softness or hardness.

Procedure

1. Prepare 1 liter of each of the hard and soft water benchmark solutions. The benchmark solutions will be of 5 different grades of distilled water containing the calcium chloride—a soft water solution (containing 0–17.1 mg/l), a slightly hard water solution (17.1–60 mg/l), a moderately hard water solution (60–120 mg/l), a hard water solution (120–180 mg/l), and a very hard water solution (180+ mg/l). *Note: you can convert mg/l into grains per gallon by dividing the amount of mg/l by 17.1.*

2. Pour each solution into a separate test tube, filling it ⅓ of the way up.

3. Drop 1 drop of liquid hand soap into each test tube with the pipette. Cap the tubes with the stoppers and shake vigorously for 10 seconds each. Then use a black marking pen to indicate the highest point on the test tube that the bubbles reached. These will become your benchmark samples. Place them in a test tube rack.

4. Take the first sample of tap water to be tested and pour it ⅓ of the way up in a test tube. Drop 1 drop of liquid hand soap into the test tube and shake vigorously for 10 seconds. Then, with the black marking pen, indicate the highest point on the test tube that the bubbles reached. Repeat this step for each water sample.

5. Once all of your water samples are tested, compare the amount of bubbles generated in each sample test tube with those of the benchmark test tubes and match the sample results with similar results obtained from the bench-mark group. Record your observations. For example, if one water sample produced the same amount of bubbles as a benchmark tube that contains minerals that are between 120–180 mg/l, then record this observation with your estimate that the water in your sample is probably hard water.

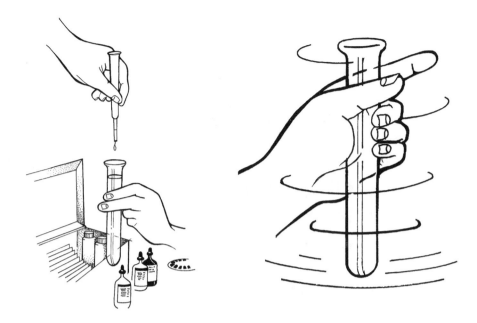

Once the hard and soft water solution test tubes have been prepared, a drop of liquid hand soap will be introduced into each tube. Then each tube will be capped. Shake vigorously for 10 seconds and mark the highest point on each tube that the soap bubbles reached to create your benchmark samples.

6. Once you have compared all of your water samples, perform the actual hard water test on each sample with the test kit. There are various test kits on the market for this procedure. Probably the easiest one to use is a drop titration kit. Follow the directions for testing hard water that comes with the test kit. Record your results.

7. Now compare the actual results with the results you obtained from the bubble test and note your results.

Results

1. In the benchmark group of water samples was there a measurable difference between the amount of bubbles formed in the soft water and in the hard water?

2. How did the bubbles from the tap water samples obtained from well water sources compare to the benchmark group?

3. How did the bubbles from the tap water samples obtained from public water supply sources compare to the benchmark group?

4. What were the actual results obtained from the hard water test kit? Did these results corroborate the results you obtained from your bubble test?

18

Can Pascal's Triangle Be Found in Various Graphs and Patterns in Various Situations?

Note: In order to understand and perform this project, knowledge or research on the subject of Pascal's triangle is required.

Purpose

To apply Pascal's triangle to different situations and determine the following: (1) if the digital root patterns of Pascal's triangle by row compare to the digital root patterns of other number groups such as multiples of 2, 3, 5, and so on, and to odd and even digital root patterns; (2) if there are similar patterns on the graph of EKG readings and the graph of the digital roots of Pascal's triangle by row upside down; (3) if there are similar patterns on the graph of EEG readings and the digital roots of Pascal's triangle by row right side up; (4) if there are visual patterns in the shaded multiples of numbers in the digitally rooted Pascal's triangle; (5) if there are similar patterns on the graph of seismogram readings of an earthquake and the graph of the digital roots of Pascal's triangle by row right side up; (6) if there are similar patterns on the graph of the seismogram reading of sound waves and the graph of the digital roots of Pascal's Triangle by row right side up; and (7) if there are any similar patterns on the graphs of the spectra of the sun, a quasar, and an unknown object from space and the digital roots of Pascal's triangle.

Hypothesis

Pascal's triangle (as shown in the figure below) is a fascinating mathematical study brought to light by Blaise Pascal in the 1600s. It contains many interesting numerical and mathematical patterns that are too detailed to list here. The patterns created within this triangle seem endless and it is possible that these patterns may exist in different grids and in nature.

Materials Needed

- blank Pascal's triangle
- graph paper
- original Pascal's triangle on paper
- calculator (if necessary)
- ruler
- graph of the digital roots of Pascal's triangle by row
- graph of EKG readings (may be obtained from your family doctor)
- graph of EEG readings (may be obtained from your family doctor)
- graph of a seismogram reading of an earthquake
- graph of sound waves
- graphs of the spectra of the sun, a quasar, and an unknown object from space

Pascal's Triangle

Procedure

Study 1

1. Research Pascal's Triangle to understand how it works and the calculations and patterns that can be found within it. Then take a blank copy of Pascal's Triangle and turn each number on it into its digital root.

2. On a piece of graph paper, label the vertical axis "Value of Digital Root," starting at 0 and ending at 9.

3. On the same piece of graph paper, label the horizontal axis by the name of the group of numbers chosen.

4. Take the same graph and choose a number group to graph.

5. Take the digital roots of the number graph and graph them using a line graph form.

6. Continue the graph until a pattern appears or nothing has appeared to a point where you choose not to graph anymore.

7. Once you are done graphing all of the number groups chosen, compare them and see if there are similar patterns found in any of them

8. Draw your conclusions.

Study 2

Place the graph of the digital roots of Pascal's triangle upside down next to the graphs of the EKG readings and compare for similar patterns on each.

Study 3

Place the graph of the digital roots of Pascal's triangle right side up next to the graphs of the EEG readings and compare for similar patterns on each.

Study 4

Take a blank copy of the digitally rooted Pascal's triangle and select a number group to shade (e.g., multiples of 2, 3, 4, etc., or odd or even numbers). Shade in the digital roots that belong to the number group selected and record the results. Repeat the process for each number group.

Study 5

Take the graph of the digital roots of Pascal's triangle and place it right side up next to the graph of the seismogram readings. Compare for similar patterns on each.

Study 6

Place the graph of the digital roots of Pascal's triangle right side up next to the sound waves graph. Compare for similar patterns on each.

Study 7

Place the graph of the digital roots of Pascal's triangle next to the graphs of the spectra of the sun, a quasar, and an unknown object from space and look for any similar patterns.

Results

1. Did patterns appear in any of the studies? What types of patterns did you find?
2. What practical applications might Pascal's triangle have in the real world?

19

Do Aluminum Pots, Pans, and Foil Leach Aluminum to Acidic Foods Cooked in These Mediums?

Note: This project requires the use of materials and equipment found in a chemistry laboratory. The student will need to work with a mentor who is a chemistry research scientist or a graduate student who can assist with performing certain procedures and operating various equipment.

Purpose

To determine whether cooking acidic foods in aluminum pots, pans, and foil will cause aluminum to leach into the foods, thereby possibly contributing to a person's intake of aluminum.

Hypothesis

We are all exposed to aluminum, which is a useful metal found abundantly in our environment. However, many studies have shown that aluminum entering the human body has long-term negative health effects and is often associated to neurodegenerative diseases such as Alzheimer's disease. Since many people cook with aluminum pots and pans, as well as aluminum foil, they may be putting themselves at risk of ingesting unwanted aluminum.

Materials Needed

- aluminum pot or pan
- 1 gallon distilled water
- ½ cup white vinegar
- stove with oven
- 8 sterile 50-ml graduated cylinders with stoppers

- dish detergent (to clean pot between tests)
- ½ cup lemon juice
- 2 sliced tomatoes
- aluminum foil
- ascorbic acid powder pillow
- test tubes
- AluVer 3® aluminum reagent powder pillow
- stoppers for the test tubes
- Bleaching 3 reagent powder pillow

Equipment Needed

- spectrophotometer

Experiment

Various acidic food items will be combined with distilled water and boiled separately in the aluminum pot for a set period of time. As a control, distilled water will be boiled alone in the aluminum pot. Aluminum foil will be molded into bowl shapes and filled with the various acidic food items combined with distilled water. These bowls will then be placed in an oven at 350°F for a set period of time. As a control, distilled water will be placed alone in the aluminum foil bowl. Samples of all the boiled and heated liquids will be tested for the presence of aluminum using the AluVer 3® aluminum reagent powder pillow. If any samples test positive, the quantity of aluminum contained within them will be determined through the use of the spectrophotometer.

Procedure

1. Take the aluminum pot or pan and fill it with 2 cups of distilled water. Then add ¼ cup of white vinegar to the water and place the pot on a stove. Turn the stove burner on high and allow the solution to "cook" for 30 minutes. At the end of the 30 minutes, turn off the heat source and let the liquid cool. Pour the contents into a graduated cylinder up to the 50 ml line and stopper the sample. Label the sample. Throw away any leftover liquid. Repeat this step using a sliced tomato instead of the vinegar. Pour the contents into the graduated cylinder for this sample, stopper, and label. Repeat this step again using ¼ cup of lemon juice and then repeat with the distilled water alone (the control).

2. Preheat the oven to 350°F. Take a large sheet of aluminum foil and mold it into the shape of a bowl that can contain 2 cups of water without leaking. Pour a cup of water into the aluminum foil bowl and add ¼ cup of the white vinegar. When the oven reaches 350°F, place the aluminum foil bowl in the oven and leave it there for 30 minutes. At the end of the 30 minutes, take the bowl out of the oven, let the liquid cool, carefully pour the liquid into a graduated cylinder, stopper and label the sample. Repeat this step, first with a sliced tomato instead of the vinegar, then with lemon juice, and finally with the distilled water by itself.

3. Collect all samples together.

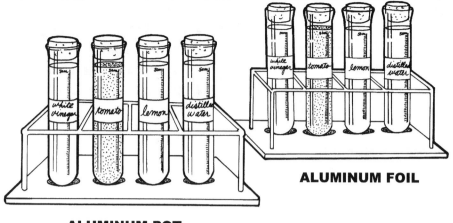

ALUMINUM FOIL

ALUMINUM POT

Liquid samples of boiled liquids from the aluminum pot and foil.

4. In the chemistry laboratory, turn on the spectrophotometer and allow the equipment to warm up. Your mentor will show you how to set the wavelength, adjust the display, and set the mode for later testing of the samples.

5. Take your first sample. Empty one ascorbic acid powder pillow (used to remove any interference of the results caused by iron) into the graduated

Add the ascorbic acid powder pillow and the Aluver 3 aluminum reagent powder pillow into the graduated cylinder for a sample liquid and then add the bleach powder pillow.

Stopper and shake vigorously and note the color of the sample for the presence of aluminum.

cylinder and swirl around the contents of the cylinder a few times until the powder is dissolved.

6. Empty the contents of one AluVer 3® aluminum reagent powder pillow into the graduated cylinder and place the stopper on top. Swirl or invert the cylinder several times for about 1 minute to completely dissolve the powder.

7. Pour 25 ml of the sample into a test tube and set aside. Add one Bleaching 3 reagent powder pillow to the 25 ml in the cylinder and place the stopper on top. Shake vigorously for 30 seconds.

8. If aluminum is present in the sample, it will turn a red-orange color. The darker the color, the more aluminum present in the sample.

9. If aluminum is present in a sample, transfer some of the 25ml sample into a test tube that you set aside in step 7. With the help of your mentor, place it in the spectrophotometer to read the concentration of aluminum in the prepared sample.

10. Record your results.

11. Repeat steps 5–10 with all the other samples.

Results

1. Did any of the samples collected test positive for the presence of aluminum? If so, identify the samples and note the color of the test solution.

2. If any specimens tested positive for the presence of aluminum, what concentrations of aluminum did you record?

20

Does Killing Soil Microorganisms Result in Better Plant Growth

Purpose

To determine if soil that has had its microorganisms destroyed is better for growing plants than soil that still contains microorganisms.

Hypothesis

Numerous types of microorganisms are found in various types of soil. Sometimes bacteria and other microorganisms in soil are useful in the biodegradability of certain harmful elements such as chemicals that may be present in the soil; however, sometimes bacteria and other microorganisms, through metabolism, can increase the toxicity of chemicals and can sometimes be harmful to plants. Therefore, killing bacteria and other microorganisms found in soil might be beneficial to the growth of plants.

Materials Needed

- 12 cups soil (6 cups of topsoil from a nursery and 6 cups from your lawn or a friend's lawn that has been treated with fertilizer)
- 12 8-ounce clay pots
- 2 plastic microwaveable trays
- microwave oven

- tomato plant seeds
- bean plant seeds
- pumpkin seeds
- 12 plastic bags
- water

Experiment

Two different soil types, one from a lawn that has been treated with fertilizer and one that is rich natural topsoil, will each be tested. Half of each soil sample will be subjected to microwaves, which will be used to kill any microorganisms that may be present in either soil sample. Then tomato, bean, and pumpkin seeds will be grown in each variety of treated and untreated soil sample. The progress of the growth of each of these seeds as they sprout and grow will be monitored and compared to determine if killing the organisms present in either soil sample prior to planting the seeds had a positive effect on the growth of the plants.

Procedure

1. Take 3 cups of soil from the fertilized lawn and 3 cups of the nursery topsoil and place 1 cup of each into one of the clay pots. (These 6 soil samples will serve as a control.)

2. With the remaining fertilized lawn soil and nursery topsoil samples, take 3 cups of each, place them on different trays, and label them accordingly.

3. Take the fertilized lawn soil sample tray and place it in the microwave oven. Turn the microwave on "high" for 10 minutes.

4. Remove the tray from the oven and allow the soil to cool to room temperature. Then put 1 cup of the soil from the cooled tray into each of 3 pots and label the pots.

5. Repeat steps 3–4 for the nursery topsoil sample.

6. Once the different soil samples are in their pots, evenly distribute the tomato, bean, and pumpkin seeds into each of the 12 marked pots. Water the soil in the pots and cover the pots with plastic bags.

7. Give the plants the required amount of water each day according to instructions found on the seed packets in order to germinate the seeds.

Place half of each soil sample into the microwave oven and heat on "high" for 10 minutes.

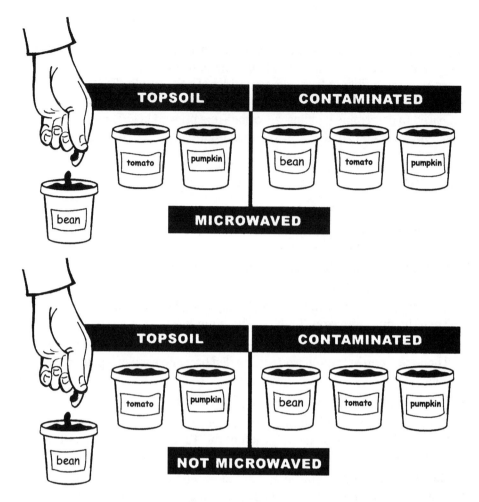

8. Once sprouts are observed above the soil line of the pots, remove the plastic bags and allow the plants to grow. Be sure to provide the plants with an equal amount of water and sunlight for each seed type according to growing instructions found on the seed packets for that type of seed.

9. Carefully monitor and note the progress of the plants over a 2-month period. Then compare the growth results among the plants in the various soil types.

Results

1. How did the plants that grew in all samples of the fertilized lawn soil compare to all plants grown in the nursery topsoil samples?

2. How did the plants that grew in the normal fertilized lawn soil and nursery top soil samples compare to those that were grown in the microwaved soil samples, overall?

3. Does treating the soil with microwaves to kill microorganisms appear to have a positive or negative effect on plant growth?

4. Which group of tomato plant seeds flourished the best? Which group of bean plants flourished the best? Which group of pumpkin seeds flourished the best?

21

Which Type of Flame Retardant Is Most Effective in Reducing the Flammability of an Evergreen Tree?

Note: Adult supervision is required for this project and caution should be exercised when handling the tree branches in the fire source. You should look for a firefighter or certified fire management professional in your community who will be able to mentor you with this project and help apply the various fire retardants. The handling of fire retardants must comply with applicable local, state, and federal regulations, which your mentor can guide you through. Finally, for projects involving this type of substance, you will need to complete additional forms for the prescreening of your project and approval by a scientific review committee authorized by your state or regional science fair prior to the start of your research.

Purpose

To determine which form of fire retardant works best in reducing the flammability of an evergreen tree.

Hypothesis

Severe forest wildfires have become a problem for the vegetation, climate, and topography in the western United States as well as in other parts of the world in recent years. In certain cases, fire retardants have proven useful in slowing the spread of fires. Although most fire retardants contain nitrogen and phosphorus as their main ingredients, they also contain other ingredients. Additionally, fire retardants are available in powder, gel, and liquid forms. Therefore, certain forms of fire retardants might work better than others.

Materials Needed

- 12 evergreen tree limbs, 2–3 feet in length, of, for example, pine, balsam, and cedar
- nonflammable protective clothing
- nonflammable protective gloves
- goggles or other protective eyewear
- fire source (a large wood-burning fireplace is best)
- fire retardant powder
- fire retardant gel
- fire retardant liquid
- water
- large bucket
- large metal tongs
- large metal bucket filled with cold water
- fire extinguisher

Experiment

Three sets of various evergreen tree branches will be treated individually with three different fire retardants and held with tongs in a fire source to determine which fire retardant appears to be the most effective in preventing the branches from catching fire. Then another set of evergreen tree beaches not treated with fire retardant will be held with tongs in a fire source to serve as a control.

Procedure

1. Contact a local firefighter or certified fire management professional in your area who will be able to supervise and mentor you while you perform your experiment and recommend and/or check the safety of the fire source you will use to test your treated tree limbs.

2. Collect 12 evergreen tree branches (4 of each from a different type of evergreen tree) that are each 2–3 feet in length. Choose branches that can be held firmly with a pair of long tongs at a safe distance from the fire source while they are being exposed to the fire source, and can be dropped completely and safely into the fire source if they catch fire (for safety).

3. Label each branch with the type of evergreen tree that it came from and the type of fire retardant it will be treated with, for example, "Pine-Powder," "Pine-Gel," "Pine-Liquid," "Pine-Control," "Balsam-Powder," "Balsam-Gel," "Balsam-Liquid," "Balsam-Control," "Cedar-Powder," "Cedar-Gel," "Cedar-Liquid," and "Cedar-Control."

4. With the advice and assistance of your mentor, select a commercial brand of fire retardant powder, gel, and liquid that can be applied to the tree limbs for testing.

5. According to the recommendations of your mentor, dress appropriately for the experiment in safe attire along with gloves and protective eyewear.

6. Collect your test branches, identify a safe, effective fire source, select the commercial brands of fire retardant that you will test, and obtain the appropriate safety attire. Then you will be ready to get started.

An evergreen branch being treated with one of the fire retardant substances.

7. Start the flame in your fire source.

8. Test the fire retardant powder. With the help of your mentor, mix the powder with the required amount of water in the large bucket. When the powder mixture is prepared, take the first branch and dip it in the bucket of the mixture, being sure to cover as much of the branch as possible that will be exposed to the flame source.

9. Use the tongs to firmly pick up the first branch to be tested from the bucket. Hold the branch firmly and expose it to the fire source for two minutes while rotating the branch around in the fire. Carefully monitor the branch during this time to see if catches fire at all. If the branch catches fire, note how long it took to catch fire. After two minutes take the branch out of the fire and carefully place it hot side down into the metal bucket of cold water. If at any time the branch catches fire, carefully drop the branch into the wood fireplace (if using one) or have your mentor extinguish the fire with the fire extinguisher.

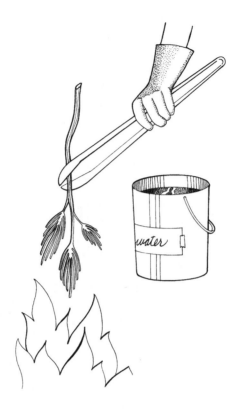

With the help of your supervisor, carefully use the tongs to firmly pick up a branch and expose it to the fire source.

10. Repeat step 9 for the two other different evergreen tree branches and note your results.
11. Test the fire retardant gel. With the help of your mentor, apply the gel evenly to each of the 3 different types of evergreen tree branches.
12. Repeat step 9 and note your results.
13. Test the fire retardant liquid. With the help of your mentor, apply the liquid evenly to each of the 3 different types of evergreen tree branches.
14. Repeat step 9 and note your results.
15. Finally, repeat steps 9–10 for each of the different branches without any fire retardant substances and note your results.

Results

1. Did any of the treated branches catch fire? If so, how long did it take before they caught fire? How did these branches compare with the control branches?
2. Which flame retardant appeared to work the best?
3. What flame retardant appears to be the most effective based on ease of application, usefulness, and cost?

22

Electromagnetic Emissions: Testing and Comparing the Nonionizing Radiation from Cellular Phones for Relative Safety

Purpose

To determine how much radiation is emitted from various makes and models of cellular phones and to compare them with the amount of radiation given off from other devices we have daily contact with—a microwave oven, a television set, and a shortwave radio.

Hypothesis

When an electric current runs through a wire or device, it produces an electromagnetic field. With many electronic devices at our disposal, we are constantly exposed to electromagnetic fields that over the long term may be harmful to the human body. Nonionizing electromagnetic radiation operates at lower frequencies and is characterized as radio frequency radiation. Emissions of this type of radiation come from devices that produce broadcast transmissions, such as cellular phones. This type of radiation has been studied and has been shown to cause thermal or heating effects on the human body that may prove to be dangerous over time. Because the widespread use of cellular phone technology is relatively new, there have been no studies to show the long-term effects of nonionizing electromagnetic radiation on people. Testing and comparing the radiation given off by cellular phones and other devices that give off radiation may give some indication of the relative safety of the devices.

Materials Needed

- CellSensor EMF detection gauss meter (an extremely low frequency [ELF] and radiation frequency [RF] gauss meter)
- various types of cellular phones (borrowed from family or friends)
- landline telephone (to call the cell phones being tested)
- microwave oven
- television
- shortwave radio

Experiment

Various cellular phones will be tested with the CellSensor EMF detection gauss meter both in use and in standby mode to determine the amount of nonionizing radiation they give off. The results will be recorded. Then the microwave oven, television, and shortwave radio will each be tested for the amount of radiation that they give off. The results obtained from the cellular phones will be compared and contrasted with those of the microwave oven, television, and shortwave radio.

Procedure

1. Fully charge each cellular phone prior to testing to ensure accurate and consistent results.

2. Turn on the CellSensor EMF detection gauss meter. (*Note:* product documentation will instruct you how to conduct a proper measurement of radiation emitted in milliwatts per centimeter (mw/cm^2) in all types of cell phones. Be sure your meter is calibrated correctly before testing any devices.

3. Take the first cell phone and turn it on. Position the CellSensor EMF detection gauss meter next to the cell phone (or as otherwise directed by the instructions) and record the radiation emission reading for the phone. Then turn the phone off to save the fully charged battery and remove excess radiation from the test area so that the results for the other phones are not affected. Repeat this step for all the other cell phones.

4. Turn on the first cell phone again. Go to your landline phone and call the number designated for this cell phone. Place the CellSensor EMF detection gauss meter next to the phone while it is ringing and record the radiation emission reading for the phone. Then answer the phone so that it is "in use." Record the radiation emission reading for the phone again after the phone stops ringing and is in "use" mode. Then turn the phone off and repeat this step for all the other cell phones.

5. Once you have obtained your data results for the cell phones, position the CellSensor EMF detection gauss meter next to the microwave oven (turned on "high" for one minute), the television set (turned on), and shortwave radio (turned on) and record the radiation emissions for these devices.

6. Compare and contrast the results obtained from the cell phones with those from the microwave oven, television set, and shortwave radio.

Place one of the cell phones to be tested next to the meter and record the radiation emission for that phone.

Results

1. What readings did you obtain from the cellular phones when turned on? What readings did you obtain when the phones were ringing and in use? Did the amounts of radiation vary between the phones when turned on? Did the amounts of radiation vary between the phones in the ringing and in-use modes? If so, was this variation significant?

2. What readings did you obtain from the microwave oven, television set, and shortwave radio? How did these readings compare with those obtained from the cell phones?

3. Do your results and studies of this subject suggest an analogy between the potential long-term effects of human body exposure to the electromagnetic fields emitted from the microwave oven, television set, and/or shortwave radio and the potential long-term effects on human body exposure to the non-ionizing radiation emitted from the cell phones?

23

Can Acid Solutions Remove Green Tones in Light-Colored Hair Caused by Copper in Swimming Pools?

Note: This project involves acquiring human hair samples. For projects involving this type of matter, you are required to complete certain forms for the pre-screening of your project and approval by a scientific review committee authorized by your state or regional science fair prior to the start of your research.

Purpose

To determine if it is possible to remove the green tones in light-colored hair caused by swimming in a pool containing copper (an alkaline) by treating the hair with solutions having various acidic pH factors.

Hypothesis

Copper is widely used in swimming pools as an effective means of eliminating algae. Copper algaecide is said to perform best at a pH of 9 or above, which makes it an alkaline. However, as useful as copper may be in controlling algae, it sometimes discolors the pool water, turns pool liners green, and, as many swimmers have found out, it also gives blond or light-colored hair green tones. It may be possible to remove the copper and therefore the green color from hair with an acidic solution that neutralizes the alkaline.

Materials Needed

- 7 swatches of natural blond hair from the same person (can be obtained from a hair salon) that are about 1 centimeter thick and 4–5 inches long
- rubber bands to hold together each hair swatch
- large bucket
- distilled water
- copper algaecide

- litmus paper and pH indicator color chart or electronic pH indicator
- 5 100-ml beakers
- 100 ml lemon juice
- 100 ml white vinegar
- 100 ml tomato juice
- 100 ml black coffee
- 100 ml milk

Experiment

Various swatches of naturally blond hair that have not been colored or chemically treated will be submersed in a bucket containing a solution of water and copper algaecide with a pH level of 9 for one hour. The swatches will then be removed, rinsed, and allowed to dry. Later they will be submersed in various solutions containing different acid pH levels. The color of the hair swatches will be monitored to observe any changes that occur to neutralize their color back to its original and natural tone.

Procedure

1. Make arrangements with a hair salon to obtain 7 different swatches of naturally blond hair (from the same person to achieve consistent results). Gather the swatches of hair into bundles of about one centimeter each and bind each one separately with a rubber band.
2. Fill a bucket halfway with distilled water and add enough of the copper algaecide to achieve a pH of 9 on the litmus paper color indicator chart or on the electronic pH meter.
3. Submerse six of the banded hair swatches into the bucket and leave them in the bucket for an hour. Periodically stir the liquid in the bucket to make sure the copper does not separate from the water. The remaining hair swatch will be used as a reference to compare with the hair color of the other swatches at the end of the experiment.
4. After one hour, remove each hair swatch, rinse, and allow to dry. The swatches should have green tones in them.
5. Fill one of the 100-ml beakers with 100 ml of lemon juice (most acidic with an average pH of 2.0), one with 100 ml of white vinegar (second most acidic with an average pH of 2.5), one with 100 ml of tomato juice (moderately acidic with

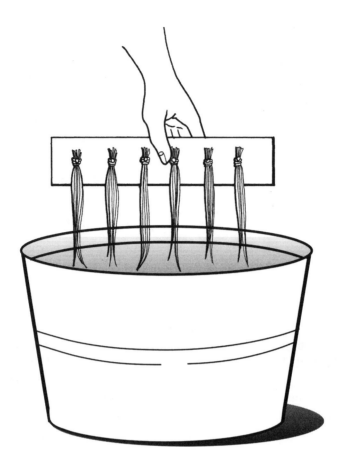

Submerge 6 of the 7 hair swatches into the bucket of water and copper algaecide for one hour.

an average pH of 4.0), one with 100 ml of black coffee (less acidic with an average pH of 5.0), one with 100 ml of milk (the least acidic with an average pH of 6.5), and finally, as a control, one with 100 ml of distilled water (with a neutral pH of 7.0). Verify the exact pH levels for each solution with the litmus paper test or electronic pH indicator.

6. Take the hair swatches treated with the copper algaecide and place one swatch into each of the five test beakers and one into the control beaker containing the distilled water.

7. Allow all the swatches to remain in the solutions for one hour.

8. After one hour, remove each hair swatch, rinse, and allow to dry.

9. Take the hair swatch that was not subjected to the copper algaecide and use it as a basis from which to compare the six swatches that were subjected to the copper algaecide to see which, if any, hair swatch color was neutralized closest to the original natural color.

After the experimental set of hair swatches has been removed from the copper algaecide and allowed to be rinsed and dried, place one of each into the test beakers containing various acidic solutions for one hour and remove them to see if green tones are eliminated from the swatches.

Results

1. Which acidic sample was the most effective in removing the green tones from the hair samples?

2. Did any acidic sample completely remove the green tones from the hair swatches? Did the stronger, moderate, or weaker acids do a better job?

3. Does there appear to be a correlation between the strength of the pH level of the acid and the pH level of the base copper algaecide solution in removing green tones and therefore neutralizing the pH of the hair?

24

Which Environment Harbors the Most Antibiotic-Resistant Bacteria?

Note: This project involves testing with pathogenic bacteria and working with antibiotics. For projects involving these types of materials, you are required to work with a research scientist as your mentor and complete additional forms for the prescreening of your project and approval by a scientific review committee authorized by your state or regional science fair prior to the start of your research.

Purpose

To determine whether a hospital, school, or private home has the most antibiotic-resistant bacteria and which antibiotic, if any, appears to be resisted the most by bacteria found in these environments.

Hypothesis

Bacterial resistance to certain antibiotics has posed serious concerns in recent years. Because of the overuse and misuse of antibiotics, some bacteria have developed a resistance by altering their cell walls or their ribosomes, or by transferring plasmids between bacteria, as well as through other means. Bacteria in certain environments, such as hospitals, may be more resistant to antibiotics than bacteria in other environments, and they may be more resistant to some antibiotics than others.

Materials Needed

- disposable gloves
- petri dishes: tryptic soy agar (TSA) with 5% sheep blood (available at scientific supply stores)
- sterile applicators
- bacteria from sinks in a hospital, school, and private home

- incubator
- wooden sticks
- calibrated vials
- nutrient broth (available at scientific supply stores)
- sterile forceps
- sterile filter paper disks impregnated with antibiotics

(consult with your mentor for the types of antibiotics you will use, for example, tetracycline, ampicillin, erythromycin, cippron, and cephalothin)
- metric ruler

Experiment

Visits will be made to hospitals, schools, and private homes to obtain several bacterial cultures from bathroom sinks at these sites. The bacteria will then be transferred and grown on TSA petri dishes containing 5% sheep's blood, and then subcultured and grown in nutrient solutions for two hours. Then, they will be cultured on TSA petri dishes containing 5% sheep's blood. Filter paper disks impregnated with different types of antibiotics will be placed on petri dishes containing subcultures of bacteria from all the sites visited. The petri dishes will be incubated at 35°C for 24 hours. Observations will be made to determine whether the bacteria cultured from these sites were killed or resisted any of the antibiotics. The results between the sites will be compared along with each antibiotic.

Procedure

1. Obtain permission from the management of each site and private home visited to take bacteria cultures from the bathroom sinks.

2. Once you have authorization, put on your gloves and take the petri dishes and sterile applicators with you (enough to obtain a number of samples from a particular sink that matches the number of antibiotics you will be testing later in the experiment; for example, if you plan to test 5 different antibiotics then be sure to obtain 5 petri dish samples from the same sink site). Swab the sinks with separate sterile applicators and streak them onto separate petri dishes. Cover the dishes with sterile covers and label them with the name of the source each sample came from.

3. Incubate the petri dishes for 24 hours at 35°C.

4. Remove the petri dishes and select various strains of bacteria found on each dish. Subculture these bacteria on separate petri dishes at 35°C for another 24 hours.

5. Remove two colonies of bacteria from each petri dish with sterile wooden sticks and place them in individual calibrated vials filled with 4 ml of nutrient broth. Incubate for 2 hours at 35°C.

6. At the end of the 2 hours, streak the contents onto new petri dishes with separate sterile applicators.

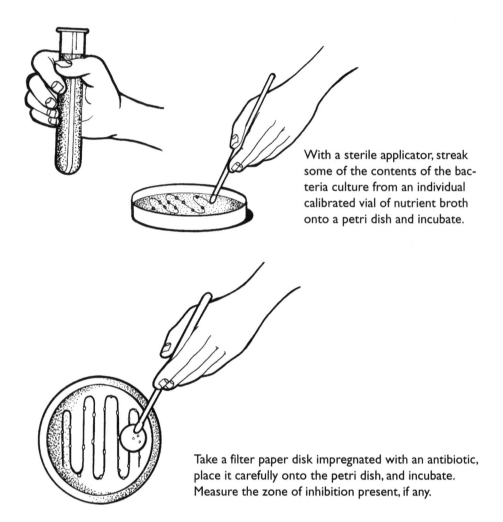

With a sterile applicator, streak some of the contents of the bacteria culture from an individual calibrated vial of nutrient broth onto a petri dish and incubate.

Take a filter paper disk impregnated with an antibiotic, place it carefully onto the petri dish, and incubate. Measure the zone of inhibition present, if any.

7. With the sterile forceps, take the disks impregnated with antibiotics and place one on the surface of each petri dish so that the disks will diffuse into the medium. Then incubate the petri dishes for two hours at 35°C.

8. Analyze each petri dish for the existence of bacteria to determine if the bacteria are antibiotic resistant. Measure the zones of inhibition with the ruler and record your data. A zone of inhibition is the clear region around the disk in which no bacterial growth has occurred.

Results

1. Which site had the most bacteria? Which site had the least? Were the bacteria killed when treated with antibiotic impregnated disks as evidenced by any zones of inhibition?

2. Which site, if any, had antibiotic-resistant bacteria? Which antibiotics did this bacteria resist? If multiple sites had antibiotic-resistant bacteria, were the bacteria obtained from these sites resistant to the same types of antibiotics?

25

Do Earthworms Affect the Level of Nitrates and Phosphates Found in Fertilized Soil?

Purpose

To determine whether adding earthworms to fertilized soil will decrease levels of phosphates and nitrates found in fertilized soil.

Hypothesis

Fertilizer contains certain amounts of nitrates and phosphates that help lawns grow and look healthy. However, overuse of fertilizer can result in groundwater contamination. Earthworms may be effective in reducing the levels of nitrates and phosphates in soil.

Materials Needed

- 24 cups of potting soil
- measuring cups
- 2 large clear plastic containers with small holes on bottom for aeration
- soil fertilizer for potting soil
- 1 cup of ground fruit or vegetables
- distilled water
- Rapitest® soil test kit
- 20 earthworms

Experiment

Soil fertilizer, which raises the levels of phosphates and nitrates in soil, will be added to 2 containers of potting soil. The level of nitrates and phosphates present in the soil in each container will be tested and recorded. Then earthworms will be added to one container. The other container will not have any earthworms and will serve as a control. Both containers will be tested at the end of each week for a one-month period to find the level of nitrates and phosphates in each container's soil and to determine if the worms have decreased the level of phosphates and nitrates in the soil.

Procedure

1. Add 12 cups of the potting soil to each of the 2 clear plastic containers.
2. Add the recommended amount of soil fertilizer for 12 cups of soil to container 1 and mix well. Repeat for container 2.
3. Container 1 will serve as the control. It will contain no earthworms and will be put aside.
4. Mix ground fruit or vegetables into the soil of container 2.
5. Add 1 cup of distilled water to each container and mix so that the soil in each container is damp.
6. Use the Rapitest® soil test kit to test for the amount of phosphates and nitrates in container 1 and container 2 prior to beginning the experiment. Follow the directions that come with the kit.
7. Once you have tested the level of phosphates and nitrates present in the soil samples, you are ready to test the effects of the worms. Add 20 earthworms to container 2 and leave them in the container for one month.

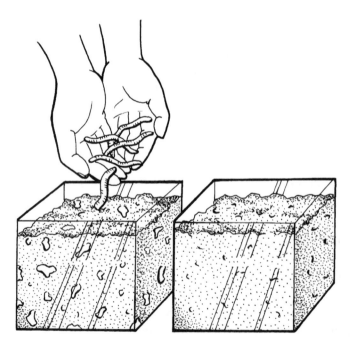

Add 20 earthworms to the experimental container to determine if they affect the level of nitrates and phosphates in the soil.

8. Add 1 cup of distilled water each day to each container to keep the soil consistently damp.

9. At the end of each week, repeat step 6 on both containers.

10. Compare your recorded data results of the level of nitrates and phosphates present in the soil samples for each week to see if they changed when the worms were added to the soil in container 2.

Results

1. What were the levels of nitrates and phosphates in the soil samples of each container prior to the start of the experiment?

2. What were the level of nitrates and phosphates in the soil samples of each container at the end of each week?

3. Did the level of nitrates and phosphates decrease in the soil samples from the container with the worms?

26

Can Canker Be Transmitted to Healthy Trees through Infected Soil?

Purpose

To determine if canker will spread in a controlled environment through soil transmission to noninfected trees.

Hypothesis

Canker is a disease to which many types of trees are susceptible and is caused by a fungus. It is a serious disease that will kill an infected tree unless it is treated quickly and efficiently. Typically the disease attacks a tree if it is injured or weakened in a particular spot or subjected to environmental stresses. The disease is known to spread by one tree coming in contact with the tissue of another tree infected by the disease and also through airborne transmission or by visiting insects. It may also be transmitted through soil.

Materials Needed

- 3 plum trees from a nursery
- 3 planting pots (8x5.5 with holes on the bottom)
- 3 pounds of cow manure
- nine pounds of a regionally formulated organic soil ideal for growing plum trees (from a nursery)
- water
- knife
- 6 ounces of soil that was around a tree infected by canker (*Note:* Canker can be caused by different types of fungus; therefore, it is necessary to research the symptoms and outward signs evidencing the presence of canker so that you can locate and identify a suitable soil sample.)
- greenhouse or solarium to grow the trees (You may need to contact a mentor from a nursery or agricultural school to obtain access to a greenhouse.)

Experiment

Three plum trees will be planted in pots that each contain the same amounts of soil and cow manure. Each tree will then be given the same amount of time to adjust to the potted soil in a greenhouse or solarium. One tree will be wounded by a knife and remain in the greenhouse or solarium and another will be moved to an environment that is colder than the greenhouse/solarium habitat. The remaining tree will stay in the greenhouse or solarium. Then each plant will receive 2 ounces of canker-infected soil. Observations will be made daily for the presence of canker on all the trees over a period of 60 days.

Procedure

1. Obtain 3 plum trees from a local nursery. Label them Plant A, Plant B, and Plant C.
2. Put a 1-inch thick layer of cow manure at the bottom of each pot. Place 3 pounds of soil in each pot and plant 1 tree in each pot. Water the plants.
3. Put the trees in a temperature-controlled greenhouse or solarium and water accordingly. Give each tree one week to adapt to its new environment. Observe the condition of the plants during this period.
4. At the start of the second week, take the knife and wound Plant A by gouging a portion of its stem or by dragging the knife vertically along its stem for one to two inches. (Remember, the purpose of this step is to create a wound that will normally heal on a plant. Do not create a wound that will kill the plant.) Take Plant B and bring it outside so that it is subjected to a colder temperature and weather elements. Leave Plant C in the greenhouse or solarium. Continue to water the plants accordingly. Observe the condition of the plants for the next week.

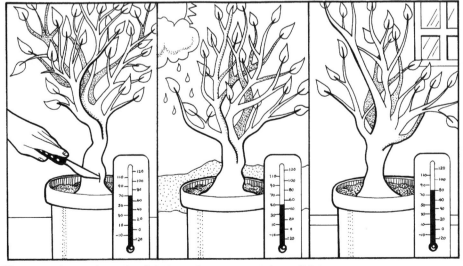

The potted trees in each of their environments and conditions.

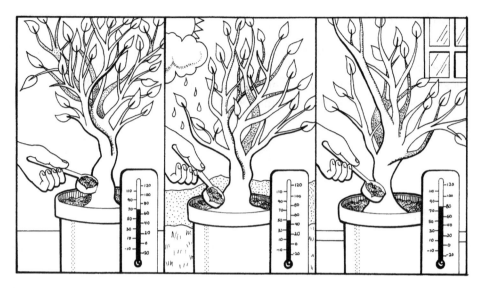

The potted trees being subjected to the canker soil in their different environments and conditions.

5. At the start of the third week, take 2 ounces of the infected soil and thoroughly mix it into the soil of each of the potted plants. Continue to water the plants accordingly.

6. Carefully observe each planting for a 2-month period to see if any of the trees become infected from the soil and to determine if a healthy tree exposed to canker-infected soil will acquire the disease, or whether wounds and stress on a tree are imperative for a tree to acquire the disease.

Results

1. Did any of the trees show symptoms of being infected by canker? If so, what did you observe? How did it form?

2. If any trees became infected, what was the first tree to acquire the disease? What tree appeared to be the least affected by the canker-infected soil?

3. What was the condition of the healthy tree? Does tree health seem to have an impact on preventing the onset of canker?

27

What Is the Growth Rate of Mold among Protein, Fat, and Carbohydrate Food Products?

Purpose

To determine which food type will form mold the fastest under different conditions.

Hypothesis

When food loses its freshness, it begins to break down and decay. One of the ways this happens is through the growth of mold on the food. Moldy food is no longer edible and must be discarded. Knowing the average length of time foods remain fresh and when they ought to be replenished can help a household budget and manage its supply of fresh food more efficiently. To this end, it would be helpful to determine the growth rates of molds on certain foods in different environments.

Preparing the various foods for testing.

Materials Needed

- fresh strawberries
- fresh cucumber
- cheddar cheese
- 3 eggs
- potato
- bread
- slice of raw roast beef
- sour cream
- 24 sterile plastic petri dishes
- labels
- plastic bags
- refrigerator with a produce storage compartment
- large shoebox
- large plastic storage bin
- gloves
- surgical mask (to use when observing petri dishes)
- camera

Experiment

Sterile plastic petri dishes will be filled with various food types representing carbohydrates, proteins, and fats and will be stored in a refrigerated temperature environment, a damp room temperature environment, and a dry room temperature environment. Observations will be made daily on all specimens to determine the rate at which mold forms on each food type in different environments and in all environments in general.

Procedure

1. Cut the strawberries, cucumber, cheese, potato, bread, and roast beef into pieces. Layer the strawberries into 3 separate petri dishes and do the same with the other cut food items. Separate the egg yolks from the egg whites and lay each egg yolk in a separate petri dish. Scoop out 2 tablespoons of sour cream and layer evenly into 3 petri dishes. When finished, you should have 3 petri dishes of each food item. Be sure to cover each petri dish with its plastic lid and label each one for the food type present in each dish and the location where it will be stored.

2. Take a petri dish of each food type (group 1) and place each dish in a separate clear plastic bag. Place the plastic-covered dishes carefully into the vegetable storage compartment of a refrigerator, or another part of the refrigerator that can be used for the experiment that will not interfere with other foods in the refrigerator. An empty refrigerator (if available) would be best. Be sure that the temperature in the refrigerator is set to the normal mean temperature that your family uses to keep food cold.

3. Take the second group of petri dishes of each food type (group 2) and place them each in separate clear plastic bags. Place the plastic-covered dishes carefully in a large shoebox and store them in a dry room at room temperature.

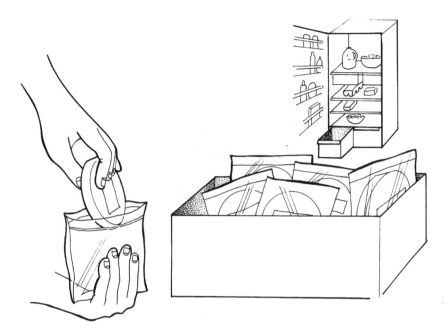

Once all of the food petri dishes are prepared, they will be placed into clear plastic bags, separated into 3 groups, and placed in different environments.

4. Take the last group of petri dishes of each food type (group 3) and place them each in separate clear plastic bags. Place the plastic-covered bags carefully in a large plastic bin and store them in a damp environment, such as a basement area.

5. Put on the gloves and observe the petri dishes daily to carefully note how each food type in each environment begins to mold and the order in which each food type in each environment begins to mold. Photograph the mold in each petri dish as soon as it becomes visible and continue to photograph the dishes until all of them fully display mold.

Results

1. Which group of petri dishes had the most mold overall? What factor in the environment of this group may have accounted for this result?

2. Which food item formed mold the quickest? Was this food a carbohydrate, protein, or fat? Was this food item also the first to form mold of all the different food types in all three environments?

3. Which type of foods seemed to form mold the fastest overall—carbohydrate, protein, or fat-concentrated foods? What factors may be responsible for this?

4. Based on your results, which types of foods should a household plan to replenish more frequently (in order to maintain freshness)?

28

Do Typology Theories on Personality Apply to Handwriting?

Note: This project involves human subjects. For projects involving people, you are required to complete additional forms for the prescreening of your project and approval by a scientific review committee authorized by your state or regional science fair prior to the start of your research.

Purpose

To determine the validity and reliability of handwriting analysis in predicting personality type.

Hypothesis

The main premise behind various typology theories is that most people can be classified according to a personality type. Various tests have been developed by psychologists over the years to characterize the personality types of people, the most popular and widely known being the Myers-Briggs Type Indicator test, which incorporates many of Carl Jung's theories on personality types. Graphology is the study of handwriting to determine various personality traits. Graphologists study letter formation in the upper, middle, and lower regions of a letter and look for various characteristics in these regions that correlate to various personality traits. Graphology has been used controversially by employers to screen potential employees and by law enforcement officials to identify character traits in individuals. Therefore, since scientists believe that the same part of the brain that controls handwriting also controls the formation of personality, there should be a correlation between typology theories and graphology.

Materials Needed

- 10 volunteers of different ages whom you know personally
- writing paper and pens
- notebook

- graphology book for interpretation and analysis of handwriting samples (or assistance by a certified graphologist who can serve as a mentor)
- 10 Myers-Briggs Type Indicator (MBTI) test booklets with instructions for administration, scoring, and interpretation of results (this test is published by Consulting Psychologists Press, Inc., of Palo Alto, California) A psychologist may serve as a helpful mentor in the use of these tests.

Experiment

Ten volunteers will be asked to give a writing sample in a set period of time. Then they will be asked to sit for a MBTI test. The handwriting samples will be collected and analyzed thoroughly for all personality characteristics and a character summary will be written up on each handwriting sample, either under the guidance of a certified graphologist or through the use of a guide book on graphology. A summary of traits for each handwriting sample will be compared and contrasted with results obtained through the MBTI test. You will also compare the results of both tests with what you know about each individual personally.

Procedure

1. Acquire 10 MBTI test booklets, answer sheets, and instructions for administering, taking, and interpreting the test results. Become familiar with the test as much as possible.

2. Arrange a time and place where you can test your volunteers. You will need to give each volunteer about 2 hours on average to complete the tests.

3. On the day of the test, distribute a sheet of paper and pen to the volunteers and have them write their name at the top of the sheet of paper. Then ask each volunteer to write as much of the Pledge of Allegiance (or the words to a song that everyone in the group knows by heart) as they can in their normal manner of writing in one minute. Let them know that they are not being tested for speed or neatness. The purpose of giving them one minute is to ensure that they will be writing in their normal writing style. When time is up, collect the writing samples.

4. Distribute a MBTI test and answer sheet to each volunteer. Be sure to have all volunteers write their name on their test answer sheet. Then read the instructions for taking the test to the volunteers and start the test. As each volunteer completes the test, collect the answer sheet and thank him or her for participating.

5. Next, with or without the help of a graphologist, analyze each handwriting sample thoroughly by studying each letter formation and looking up the stated personality trait for that letter formation. Carefully note each personality trait found for each individual in your notebook.

6. Take the MBTI test answer sheets and find the personality type of each volunteer according to the test instructions.

7. Compare the personality traits for each volunteer that you gathered from your handwriting analysis and compare them to the personality type generated for that individual from the MBTI test results. Compare the results of both tests with your observation of each individual's personality on the basis of your experience. Record your results.

Results

1. Was there a correlation between the results obtained from the handwriting personality assessment test and the results obtained from the MBTI test for each individual?

2. Did individuals with similar handwriting styles have different results on the MBTI test? Did individuals with similar MBTI test personality types have similar handwriting styles?

3. Do the composite results for either or both tests match up with the actual personality types of the volunteers based on your knowledge of these individuals?

4. Do the results of your study support or invalidate the reliability of handwriting as an indication of personality type?

29

Which Food or Beverage Provides the Most Immediate and Lasting Source of Glucose to a Hypoglycemic Person?

Note: This project involves human subjects and human tissue. For this reason you are required to complete additional forms for the prescreening of your project and approval by a scientific review committee authorized by your state or regional science fair prior to the start of your research. Additionally, you are advised to make contact with a medical doctor or other authorized medical personnel who can assist you in obtaining blood samples from the volunteers for your study and in the proper and safe handling of the blood samples.

Purpose

To determine which beverage or snack is the most ideal food source for a hypoglycemic person to consume as an immediate source of glucose that will also last the longest.

Hypothesis

Hypoglycemia, or low blood sugar, causes people to feel tired, confused, cold, headachy, and shaky. Falling blood sugar levels can even cause seizures. Hypoglycemia is often caused by a quick drop in insulin that results from skipping or delaying a meal, drinking alcohol, or even exercising. Typically, the ideal range for blood sugar levels is between 60 and 140. When blood sugar dips below 60, a hypoglycemic individual should immediately eat or drink something that contains sugar in order to raise their blood glucose levels. Therefore, since beverages and snacks contain different types of sugar in the form of complex carbohydrates to refined sugar carbohydrates, some beverages and snacks will be better than others at raising glucose levels quickly.

Materials Needed

- 3 volunteers with medically diagnosed hypoglycemia (You will need to work with a medical doctor, physician's assistant, or registered nurse who can act as a mentor to you to obtain access to volunteers, to administer various snacks, and to take blood samples from the volunteers.)
- logbook or chart to note patient information and results

- blood glucose photometric meter
- 3 bagels with butter
- 3 bowls of cooked oatmeal
- 3 oranges
- 3 glasses of vegetable juice
- 3 glasses of cola
- 3 candy bars
- water for the volunteers (if requested)

Experiment

The immediate effect of six different food sources (ranging from complex carbohydrates to fruit and vegetable carbohydrates to refined sugar carbohydrates) in raising and maintaining the blood sugar levels of three human subjects with hypoglycemia will be tested on six different occasions to determine which food source overall most efficiently provides glucose to a hypoglycemic person. In order to determine the effectiveness of a particular food source, the volunteers will have their blood sugar level measured before consuming the food source and will then have their blood sugar level measured in increments of 20 minutes after food source consumption, 60 minutes after food source consumption, and then 90 minutes after food source consumption. The results for each volunteer will be recorded and compared.

Procedure

1. Ask your family doctor or call your local hospital to make contact with a physician, physician's assistant, or registered nurse who treats hypoglycemia and would be willing to assist you in this study. They will be needed to identify the volunteers, assist you in administering the food sources, obtain the blood samples, and assist you in testing the blood samples with the blood glucose photometric meter.

2. Through your mentor identify 3 patients with hypoglycemia who would be willing to volunteer their time to participate in your study. Your mentor should determine that the volunteers are not allergic to any of the food sources being tested and that they will not experience an adverse reaction to having their finger pricked to obtain blood drop samples. Your mentor should be able to identify individuals who can participate.

3. Create a chart for each patient and note his or her name, age, weight, height, and sex at the beginning of your experiment. At the start of each test session ask your volunteers if they are experiencing any unusual events, such as stress, changes in activity or exercise levels, or sickness, which may affect the results.

4. Arrange a time and place with your mentor and volunteers where you can explain the experiment to the volunteers, administer the food sources to the volunteers, and take their blood samples. It is important that the volunteers arrive for each test on an empty stomach, having eaten nothing for 3 hours so that the results obtained will be consistent and accurate. Read the following statement to the group of volunteers: "I am conducting an experiment to see which type of food source is most effective in immediately raising your blood sugar to a normal level after consumption and which is the most effective in keeping your blood sugar at a normal level the longest after consumption. I will conduct this experiment over six different sessions on different dates for each food source tested. Each session will last about 2 hours. During this time you will be given something to eat and have your finger pricked a few times to provide blood samples that will be used to measure your blood glucose levels. Thank you for your time and participation in this study."

5. Verify that that the volunteers have arrived for the test on an empty stomach, having not eaten anything for 3 hours, so that the results obtained will be consistent and accurate. Your mentor should then swab the finger of a volunteer with alcohol and collect his or her blood drop sample in a sterile blood sample test container. Label the sample with the name of the volunteer and note that it is a pretest sample. Repeat with the other volunteers.

6. Next, give each of your volunteers a bagel with butter to eat. Water can be given to the volunteers (if they desire).

7. After 20 minutes, your mentor should again swab the finger of a volunteer with alcohol and collect his or her blood drop sample into a sterile blood sample test container. Label the sample with the name of the volunteer and note that it is a "20-minute sample." Repeat with the other volunteers.

8. Repeat step 7 after 60 minutes following consumption of the bagels and after 90 minutes following consumption of the bagels. Be sure to label each sample accurately, reflecting the name of the volunteer and the time at which each sample was collected. Thank your volunteers for their time and let them know that the first session of the test has been completed.

9. With the assistance of your mentor test each sample in the blood glucose photometric meter. Carefully note the blood sugar readings in each sample for each volunteer and record your data. (*Note:* If feasible and convenient, you can test the pretest blood samples from the volunteers while they are consuming the bagels and in between the 20-, 60-, and 90-minute blood test intervals so that you can give your volunteers their blood levels for their own information.)

10. Repeat steps 5–9 with the oatmeal, oranges, vegetable juice, cola, and candy bars, each on a different test date. Record and analyze all of your results.

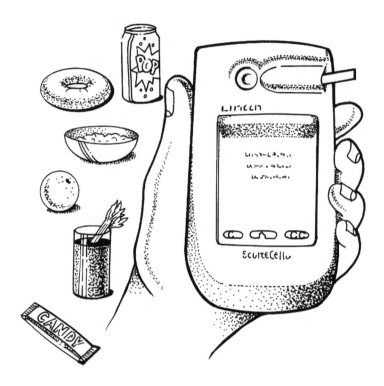

The effectiveness of various food sources in raising and maintaining blood sugar levels will be tested with a blood glucose photometric meter.

Results

1. What was the blood sugar level of each volunteer at the start of each test? Did these results vary or were they consistent?

2. Which food source delivered the quickest rise in blood sugar levels for each volunteer individually? Which food source, overall, delivered the quickest rise in blood sugar levels for the group overall?

3. Which food source seemed to sustain normal blood sugar levels the longest for each volunteer individually? Which food source seemed to sustain normal blood sugar level for the group overall? Why do you think this is the result?

30

Do Temperature and Humidity Affect the Sound of Notes Played on a Church Organ?

Note: This project requires testing a church pipe organ under different temperature and humidity conditions. Since it may be difficult to control the temperature and humidity levels immediately surrounding an organ during a fixed period of time, this experiment may need to be conducted on an organ at various phases for at least five months in order to capture different temperature and humidity levels produced by seasonal changes. Additionally, knowledge and use of an organ tuner or access to a professional organ tuner specialist are necessary to carry out this project.

Purpose

To find out which temperature and humidity level is optimal for a church pipe organ to play a note as close to the standard pipe organ pitch frequency for that note as possible and to determine how much of a pitch frequency variance there is when the temperature changes by various degrees and when humidity changes by various percentages from the optimal playing temperature and humidity level.

Hypothesis

Many church pipe organs are very old and were built at a time when churches were not heated to the standards that they are today. Newer churches have modern heating and cooling systems which have created new issues concerning heat and dryness. Changes in temperature and humidity levels are not only damaging for a church pipe organ but may also affect the consistency of the sound quality produced by the organ. Optimal temperature and humidity levels for a traditional pipe organ to produce the correct pitch can be determined, as can the amount of note frequency variance caused by changes in temperature and humidity.

Materials Needed

- traditional church pipe organ (not electronic)
- pipe organ tuning fork or tuning machine
- digital thermometer
- digital hygrometer
- notebook

Experiment

The two principal stops on a pipe organ that form the tonal basis for the entire scale of the instrument will be used. Temperature and humidity levels will be read with the thermometer and hygrometer at each visit, and the same notes will be played each time at the various octaves to determine the frequency of the notes with the tuner. The frequency readings of the notes will be compared against the true pitch frequencies for these notes. When the true pitch frequency of the notes is reached, the temperature and humidity levels present at that time will be recorded and used as the optimal temperature and humidity level from which all other temperatures, humidity levels, and frequency readings will be compared. Finally, the amount of variance that exists when the temperature changes by various degrees and when the humidity changes by various percentages will be recorded.

Procedure

1. Make arrangements with a church that has a traditional pipe organ (with a manual console and physical stops) to test and observe the temperatures, humidity levels, and pitch frequencies on the organ over a period of at least 5 months (or less if the temperature and humidity varies greatly in a shorter period of time). Additionally, make arrangements to work with a professional pipe organ tuner who may be able to mentor you in recording the frequencies of the notes played on the organ, unless you know how to measure note frequencies on an organ tuner.

2. Use the two principal stops on a pipe organ that form the tonal basis for the entire scale of the instrument (other stops can be used if desired).

3. Take the temperature in the pipe chamber of the organ with the digital thermometer and take the humidity level with the digital hygrometer. Record your readings for both.

4. With the help of your mentor (if you have one) or through your own knowledge and experience with a tuning fork or tuning machine, play the note C at various octaves and record the frequencies for each C note played. Note how far off the true pitch frequency each note is according to the tuning fork or

tuning machine. Record the frequencies for the note at each octave. You can label each note played as C1, C2, C3, C4 (middle C), and so on. Repeat with other notes at different octaves. If at any time you achieve the closest pitch frequency reading that a note should be at, remember to take note of the temperature and humidity levels present when that reading was recorded.

5. Repeat steps 1–4 at various temperature and humidity levels to achieve various readings for temperature, humidity, and frequency.

6. Analyze your data and find the variance that exists between the true pitch frequency for a note and the frequencies you recorded at various temperatures.

Results

1. Were you able to test the organ at a full range of temperatures and humidity levels? If so, at what temperature and humidity level was the organ most capable of producing frequencies that were as close as possible to the true pitch frequencies of notes played?

2. How much variance existed in the frequency of the notes played from the true pitch frequency of the notes at different temperatures and humidity levels?

31

Does Cooking Fruits and Vegetables Deplete Their Vitamin C Content?

Purpose

To determine whether cooking certain fruits and vegetables that are high in vitamin C (and are often eaten in a cooked form) will result in the depletion of vitamin C.

Hypothesis

Vitamin C is an essential vitamin for healthy skin, blood vessels, and connective tissue in the body. Vitamin C deficiency can lead to a condition called scurvy. Vitamin C is a water-soluble vitamin, meaning that it is easily dissolved in water and therefore can be found in the juices and extracts of certain fruits and vegetables. Cooking fruits and vegetables that are high in vitamin C is likely to deplete their vitamin C content.

Materials Needed

- 1 cup cherries
- 1 cup chopped tomatoes
- food blender
- cheesecloth
- 6 500-ml glass lab beakers
- burner or stove
- cornstarch
- distilled water
- 4 250-ml glass lab beakers
- 4 sterile droppers
- 2% iodine solution
- camera

Experiment

Since vitamin C is known to react with iodine, a titration test will be performed by adding iodine to a solution of a raw fruit extract mixed with a starch and then a raw vegetable extract mixed with a starch and then repeated on cooked fruit and vegetable extracts. Iodine in the solutions in excess of the amount that can be held by the vitamin C will turn the starch in the solution blue/black in color. Therefore, the color that results after the iodine is added will indicate the relative levels of vitamin C present in the fruit and vegetable extracts prior to and after cooking.

Procedure

1. Remove the pits and stems from about a cup of cherries and place the fruit in the carafe of a food processor or blender. Place the carafe into the food processor or blender to chop and pulverize the fruit. Then turn the machine off.

2. Add 150 ml of water to the fruit in the food processor or blender carafe and blend on "high" until the mixture is thoroughly blended to a liquid state.

3. Turn off the machine and strain the contents from the carafe through the cheesecloth into a 500-ml beaker. Reserve half the liquid, set aside, and label as "fruit-raw." Then take the remaining half and pour into a clean 500-ml glass lab beaker, place on a stove or burner, and heat to simmer for 15 minutes. Then set the liquid aside and label as "fruit-cooked."

4. Add 1 tablespoon of the cornstarch to a clean 500-ml beaker and add small increments of the distilled water. Mix with a clean spoon until you achieve a pastelike consistency.

5. Add 250 ml of distilled water to the cornstarch paste and bring to a boil on a burner or stove. Boil for 5 minutes.

6. Pour 75 ml of distilled water into a clean 250-ml lab beaker. Take the dropper and siphon some of the starch solution and then squeeze 10 drops of it from the dropper into the 75 ml of distilled water.

7. Take the 2% iodine solution and add incremental drops of it to the starch/water solution so that the solution turns a deep purple/indigo blue color.

8. With a clean dropper siphon some of the "fruit-raw" extract and then squeeze 10 drops of it from the dropper into the starch/iodine solution. The presence of vitamin C will cause the deep purple/indigo blue color of the starch/iodine solution to lighten in color. The lighter the color, the more vitamin C is present. Photograph the color result in the beaker.

9. Repeat steps 6–8 using the "fruit-cooked" extract. Compare the colors of the "fruit-raw" and "fruit-cooked" extracts to determine if any vitamin C was depleted during the cooking process.

10. Take the tomatoes and repeat steps 1–3 to prepare the raw and cooked vegetable extracts.

11. Repeat steps 6–9 using the vegetable extracts and photograph your results.

Siphon a portion of a test sample extract and drop into the dark blue starch/iodine solution. The presence of vitamin C in any of the test samples will cause the blue color of the starch/iodine solution to lighten in color.

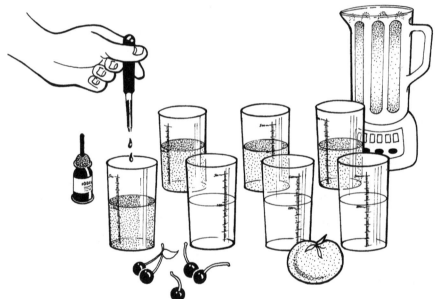

Results

1. Did the raw fruit extract show a relatively high content of vitamin C? How did it compare to the cooked fruit extract? Did the cooked fruit extract show any depletion in the content of vitamin C?

2. Did the raw vegetable extract show a relatively high content of vitamin C? How did it compare to the cooked vegetable extract? Did the cooked vegetable extract show any depletion in the content of vitamin C?

3. Which extract experienced a greater depletion after being cooked? Does this suggest that this fruit or vegetable should be eaten raw or undercooked to gain the benefits of its vitamin C?

32

Which Type of Wood Resists Water Absorption the Best in a Natural State and with Surface Coatings?

Purpose

To test a variety of different woods in a natural state for their water absorption rates and again when treated with latex paint and oil stain to see which if either of these surface coatings better reduces the water absorption rates of the various woods tested.

Hypothesis

One of the biggest concerns of homebuilders is the weathering and decay of various woods used in home construction. Water is perhaps the worst enemy of any type of wood. It can cause wood to rot, shrink, and swell, which can change the dimension of the wood, and cause paint to fail to adhere to the wood. Some types of wood may naturally absorb less water than others, and paints and stains have different effects on a wood's water absorption.

Materials Needed:

- 15 pieces of commonly used building woods cut to 3x6x½ (consisting of 3 pieces of cedar, redwood, oak, pine, and hemlock)
- 10 buckets
- water
- plastic wrap
- 1-liter graduated cylinder
- exterior latex paint
- exterior oil-based stain
- paint brushes
- paper towels

Experiment

Five pieces of wood typically used for building and construction will be tested in their natural form (untreated) by being submerged into separate buckets containing measured amounts of water for a 7-day period and covered with plastic wrap (to remove the unwanted variable of evaporation from affecting the tests results). Then the wood pieces will be removed and laid to dry on paper towels for later observation. The water remaining in each of the buckets will be measured and subtracted from the original amount of water that was added to the bucket in order to measure the amount of water absorbed by the wood in that bucket. The remaining 10 pieces of wood will be treated with the exterior latex paint and exterior oil-based stain and allowed to dry. The experiment will be repeated on each of the treated wood samples to determine the effects, if any, that the surface coatings have on water absorption by the wood.

Procedure

1. Measure 1 liter of water into each of five buckets. Carefully place one piece of wood of each type into each bucket. Label each bucket for the type of wood it will contain. Cover each bucket with plastic wrap and leave the buckets at room temperature for seven days.

2. At the end of the seventh day, carefully remove each piece of wood and allow it to drip back into the bucket for about 15 seconds. Then lay each piece of wood on paper toweling to dry.

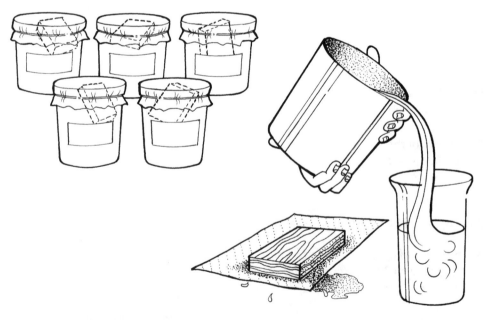

After the wood samples are removed, the water remaining in each bucket will be measured and subtracted from the original amount of water in each bucket to determine how much of it was absorbed by each sample.

3. Take the water from the first bucket, pour it into the graduated cylinder, and measure the amount of water in the cylinder. Subtract the amount of water that is in the graduated cylinder from the 1 liter that was present in the bucket at the beginning of the experiment. The amount calculated equals the amount of water absorbed by the piece of wood in the first bucket. Repeat this step for the remaining buckets and record your results.

4. Take the paint brush and paint one piece of each remaining wood type with a coating of the exterior latex paint. Allow the paint to dry. Paint the remaining pieces of each wood type with the exterior oil-based stain and allow the stain to dry. Once the samples are dry, apply one more coat of each paint or oil to the samples and allow them to dry fully.

5. Repeat steps 1–3 with the 10 treated wood samples and the 10 buckets (reuse the same 5 buckets that you used for the first group of wood samples tested) and record your results.

6. After the samples have dried, analyze the condition of all the wood samples after being exposed to the water. Note the overall condition of each piece of wood and examine for rot, shrinkage, or paint flaking, if any. Record your results.

Results

1. Of all the woods tested in their natural form, which was the most water-absorbent? Which was the most water-repellent?

2. Of all the surface coatings, which one appeared to have the most water-repellent qualities?

3. Did the most water-absorbent woods become water repellent when treated with the surface coatings?

4. What was the overall condition of each piece of wood after the experiment? Based on your results, which wood type appears to be the most durable? Is there a correlation between wood durability and water repellency?

33

Which Type of Nonmercury Body Temperature Thermometer Is the Most Accurate?

Note: This project involves human subjects. For projects involving people, you are required to complete additional forms for the prescreening of your project and approval by a scientific review committee authorized by your state or regional science fair prior to the start of your research.

Purpose

To determine which commercially available type of non–mercury containing thermometer is the most accurate for taking human body temperature, as compared to a traditional mercury thermometer that was considered the standard.

Hypothesis

Mercury has many uses, and it was the commercial standard for years in thermometers as a reliable indicator of human body temperature. However, mercury is toxic, and if it accidentally spills into the environment, it can pose a number of serious health problems for humans and wildlife. Recently laws have been passed prohibiting the sale of certain mercury-based instruments, including thermometers. Other types of thermometers have been developed to replace the old mercury thermometers. Some of the currently available alternatives may be more accurate than others as compared to a traditional mercury thermometer.

Materials Needed

- 4 volunteers of different age groups—1 child aged 9–12 years; one teen aged 15–18 years; one adult aged 25 or over; one senior adult aged 60 or over (all volunteers could come from your family)
- rubbing alcohol and sterile pads (for cleaning reusable thermometers prior to each use)
- several types of thermometers (*Note:* Some thermometers are disposable and you will need to obtain a small supply of them to conduct this experiment such as the forehead strip thermometer and the NexTemp Oral Thermometer), for example:

- ear (tympanic) thermometer
- digital thermometer
- forehead strip thermometer
- NexTemp oral thermometer (a disposable used by many school nurses)
- alcohol thermometer
- mercury thermometer (since the sale of this instrument is prohibited under various state laws, you will need to see if a family member still owns one, or you may need to work with a health care provider who may have one and may be willing to loan it to you)

Experiment

Four volunteers from four different age groups will have their temperatures taken with various types of commercially available human body thermometers and with a mercury thermometer at various points during a given day, periodically over a period of one month. The results obtained from the various thermometer readings will be recorded and compared with readings obtained from the mercury thermometer to see which alternative thermometer reads closest to the mercury thermometer, thereby providing the most accurate readings for individuals of four different age groups at different points during a given day.

Procedure

1. Choose testing days when you will have access to all of your volunteers at one point during the morning, afternoon, and evening hours.

2. On the morning of the first day of the experiment, clean the mercury thermometer thoroughly with the rubbing alcohol and sterile pads and rinse. Take extra precaution to handle the thermometer with care and avoid breaking it. Once the thermometer has been sterilized, place it in the mouth of the first volunteer. The volunteer should hold the thermometer under his or her tongue for a few minutes. Remove the thermometer to get the volunteer's body temperature reading. Record the result. Repeat this step with the other volunteers and record your results.

3. Choose the first of the other thermometer types you will be testing. Follow the directions for how to use the thermometer and take the body temperature readings of each volunteer.

4. Repeat steps 2–3 at one time during the afternoon and again in the evening. Record all mercury thermometer readings and then all test thermometer readings for all volunteers at the various times during the day.

5. Repeat steps 2–4 on a different day when all of your volunteers will be available to test a different thermometer type. Record both the mercury and test thermometer readings for all volunteers at the various times during the day.

6. Continue to repeat steps 2–4 with each of the thermometers.

Results

1. In comparison to the mercury thermometer, did the results of the test thermometers vary between each volunteer and the time of day that the readings were obtained or did they remain consistent?

2. Which commercially available test thermometer provided the closest and most consistent results as compared to the mercury thermometer?

34

A Study of the Presence of Bacteria in Moist Disposable Towelettes and Antibacterial Wipes

Purpose

To determine if a random sampling of new and partially used moist towelettes, antibacterial wipes, and their dispensers are contaminated in any way.

Hypothesis

The skin is our first line of defense that protects the rest of the body from the pathogenic bacteria present in the environment. In the course of a given day, a person's hands may encounter numerous microorganisms and bacteria that can be transferred simply through touching door handles and shaking hands. Moist towelettes and antibacterial wipes were developed to clean hands when soap and running water are not available. However, moist towelettes and even antibacterial wipes may also serve as a mechanism for the transferal of bacteria to and from the towelette dispenser.

Materials Needed

- disinfectant spray
- disposable sterile gloves
- 10 different brands of new, unused moist towelettes and antibacterial wipes in plastic dispensers
- sterile applicators
- inoculating loop
- petri dishes: tryptic soy agar (TSA) with 5% sheep blood (available from scientific supply stores)
- incubator

Experiment

Cultures will be taken from ten different brands of moist towelettes and antibacterial wipes from new containers under sterile conditions to determine whether bacteria are present. Then these containers will be given to 10 different individuals who will use the moist towelettes and antibacterial wipes for one week. At the end of the week, the dispensers will be collected from these individuals and cultures will be taken from them to determine if the used containers are hosts for bacteria.

Procedure

1. Obtain 10 different new, unused types of moist towelettes and antibacterial wipes that come in plastic dispensers.

2. Once you have collected your samples, sterilize your work area, put on the sterile gloves and open the first container of moist towelettes or antibacterial wipes. Remove the first towelette and rub a sterile applicator across the surface of the sheet. Streak the sample onto a petri dish. Cover the dish with a sterile cover and label it with the brand name of the sample.

3. Repeat step 2 for the other brands of moist towelettes and antibacterial wipes. Then close the containers of moist towelettes and antibacterial wipes and set aside.

4. Incubate the petri dishes for 48 hours at 35°C.

5. Remove the petri dishes and inspect for the presence of bacteria and record your data.

6. Take only those dispensers that tested negative for the presence of bacteria and distribute them to different individuals who work or go to school in different environments (your teachers, family members, neighbors, etc.). Tell your volunteers that they can use up to two towelettes or antibacterial wipes per day for one week and ask your volunteers to use the towelettes instead of washing their hands. Do not tell them what the purpose of the experiment is so that you do not receive any false results.

7. At the end of the week collect the dispensers from your volunteers and write the name of the volunteer on the dispenser he or she used.

8. Once again, sterilize your work area, put on the sterile gloves, and open the first container of moist towelettes or antibacterial wipes. Remove the first towelette or wipe and rub a sterile applicator across the surface of the sheet. Streak the sample onto a petri dish. Cover the dish with a sterile cover and label it with the brand of the sample and name of the person who was using it.

9. Repeat step 8 for the other brands of moist towelettes and antibacterial wipes.

10. Incubate the petri dishes for 48 hours at 35°C.

11. Remove the petri dishes and inspect for the presence of bacteria. Record your data.

Results

1. Did any of the new, unused moist towelette dispensers test positive for the presence of bacteria? What might have contributed to this result? Did any of the new, unused antibacterial wipe dispensers test positive for the presence of bacteria? What might have contributed to this result?

2. Did any of the used moist towelette dispensers test positive for the presence of bacteria? Did any of the used antibacterial wipe dispensers test positive for the presence of bacteria?

3. If any samples tested positive, interview the person(s) from whom the sample(s) came from to inquire about the conditions that surrounded their use of the product and the way they used the product.

4. If any samples tested positive, examine the shape and design of the dispensers from which the samples came and compare them to those dispensers that did not test positive to see if there is a correlation between the presence of bacteria and the shape and design of the moist towelette or antibacterial wipe dispenser.

5. Did the antibacterial wipes perform better than the moist towelettes in terms of preventing the entrance of bacteria into the dispenser?

35

The Efficacy of Oral Rinses on the Accumulation of Bacteria in the Mouth

Note: This project involves human subjects. For projects involving human subjects, you are required to work with a research scientist and complete additional forms for the prescreening of your project and approval by a scientific review committee authorized by your state or regional science fair prior to the start of your research.

Purpose

To evaluate certain oral rinses to determine whether any are effective in reducing the amount of bacteria in the mouth, both alone and in addition to brushing and flossing, and if so, how long the results last before bacteria reappear.

Hypothesis

One of the most common causes of halitosis, or bad breath, is the presence of certain bacteria in the mouth. The mouth is an ideal breeding ground for bacteria since it provides an environment that is moist and warm along with nourishment in the form of tiny bits of food that collect around the teeth. Since bacteria consume food, they also excrete waste (typically in the form of sulfur compounds), which is the cause of unpleasant mouth odors. Many commercial brands of oral rinses and mouthwashes have been designed to eliminate odors from the mouth, but are these rinses really effective in killing bacteria? Some rinses or mouthwashes may be more effective than others in killing bacteria and in preventing the regrowth of bacteria.

Materials Needed

- 12 student volunteers (6 boys and 6 girls)
- 12 toothbrushes (same brand)
- 12 tubes of toothpaste (same brand)
- 12 containers of dental floss (same brand)

- petri dishes: tryptic soy agar (TSA) with 5% sheep blood (available at scientific supply stores)
- package of plastic disposable bathroom cups
- 5 different brands of oral rinses or mouthwashes
- sterile applicators
- incubator
- sterile gloves

Experiment

Twelve students will be divided into three groups of four, with two boys and two girls in each group. They will be given instructions on the proper way to care for their teeth at home one week prior to experimental testing. After one week of following directions for proper home care, all the student volunteers will be asked to come to school each morning for one week without brushing their teeth. When they arrive at school, bacteria cultures will be taken from all the volunteers' tongues and plated onto separate petri dishes. One group will then be tested for oral bacteria after using just the rinse; the second group will be tested for oral bacteria after brushing, flossing, and rinsing; and the third group (the control) will be tested for oral bacteria after brushing and flossing only. Additional culture samples will then be taken from each group at 30- and 60-minute intervals thereafter. All bacteria samples will be labeled and incubated and the amount of bacteria present will be measured and compared. The test will be repeated every day for one week as five oral rinses are studied.

Procedure

1. Identify 12 volunteers (6 boys and 6 girls) from your class who are willing to participate in your study and are reliable enough to follow directions. Be sure to obtain permission from your science teacher or principal to perform your study during school hours with the 12 designated students and ask for a designated area to conduct the experiment.

2. Create a chart for each student and note name and sex at the beginning of your experiment.

3. Arrange a time and place to meet with your volunteers to distribute the toothbrushes, toothpastes, and dental floss. Explain the proper procedures for good oral hygiene and give them instructions on how they ought to brush their teeth, gums, and tongue and how to floss their teeth twice a day for one week prior to the start of the experiment. The purpose of this step is so that each of the volunteers will begin the study with the same standards of oral hygiene. (*Note:* Instructions for oral hygiene and proper care can be obtained from your dentist.)

4. Read the following statement to the group of volunteers: "I am conducting an experiment to see if various oral rinses are effective in eliminating bacteria in the mouth. I ask that you use the oral hygiene materials I have distributed to you in the manner that I have instructed for one week prior to the start of

the experiment. Beginning on Monday and continuing for each day of the following week, I ask that each of you bring the toothbrushes, toothpaste, and dental floss that I have given you to school and that you arrive at school each morning without brushing your teeth as I will be taking bacteria cultures from your mouth. You will then be divided into three groups. The first group will be tested using only the oral rinses; the second will be tested after brushing, flossing, and using the oral rinses; and the third group will be tested after brushing and flossing only. This will continue for the course of the week. Thank-you for your time and participation in this study."

5. Starting on the Monday of the week following the one-week, at-home oral hygiene program of the volunteers, gather your volunteers together. Put on your sterile gloves, take a sterile applicator, and gently scrape the back of the tongue of the first volunteer and streak it onto a petri dish. Then cover the dish with a sterile cover and label it with the name of the student from which the sample came. Repeat this step with the remaining volunteers.

6. Divide the volunteers into three groups of two boys and two girls each.

7. Select one of the oral rinses that will be studied (oral rinse 1). Pour oral rinse 1 into four cups and give a cup to each member of the first group (group 1). Have members of group 1 rinse their mouths with the oral rinse (as directed) and spit it into a sink. Immediately after, take a sterile applicator and gently scrape the back of the tongue of one of the group members and streak it onto a petri dish. Then cover the dish with a sterile cover and label it with the name of the student from which the sample came. Repeat with the remaining members of group 1.

8. Have members of group 2 brush and floss their teeth according to the manner that they have been instructed. Then pour oral rinse 1 into four cups and give to each member of group 2. Have all members of group 2 rinse their mouth with the oral rinse (as directed) and spit it into a sink. Immediately after, take a sterile applicator and gently scrape the back of the tongue of one of the group members and streak it onto a petri dish. Then cover the dish with a sterile cover and label it with the name of the student from which the sample came. Repeat with the remaining members of group 2.

9. Have members of group 3 brush and floss their teeth according to the manner in which they have been instructed. Immediately after, take a sterile applicator and gently scrape the back of the tongue of one of the group members and streak it onto a petri dish. Then cover the dish with a sterile cover and label the name of the student from which the sample came. Repeat with the remaining members of group 3.

10. After 30 minutes, take a sterile applicator and gently scrape the back of the tongue of one of the 12 volunteers and streak it onto a petri dish. Then cover the dish with a sterile cover and label it with the name of the student and group from which the sample came. Repeat with the remaining volunteers.

11. Repeat step 10 after another 30 minutes have passed. (*Note:* After the second 30-minute samples are obtained, members of group 1 should be allowed to brush their teeth.)

12. Take all the labeled petri dishes and incubate them at 35°C for 24 hours. Photograph the bacteria colony and carefully record the bacteria count for each student in each group daily.

13. Repeat steps 5 and 7–12 on Tuesday, using oral rinse 2. Continue to repeat this step on Wednesday, Thursday, and Friday using oral rinses 3, 4, and 5, respectively. Collect your data results and compare the effectiveness of the different oral rinses and the methods of use to see which, if any, is the most effective in eliminating bacteria.

Results

1. What was the average bacteria colony count for each student on arriving at school each morning?

2. What were the bacteria colony counts for each student in group 1 after using each of the oral rinses? What were the bacteria colony counts for each student in group 2 after using each of the oral rinses? What were the bacteria colony counts of each student in group 3 after just brushing and flossing? How much did these bacteria colony counts vary from the original bacteria colony counts obtained from the group members prior to conducting their respective oral hygiene techniques? Which oral rinse eliminated the most oral bacteria immediately after use?

3. What were the bacteria colony counts for each student 30 minutes after using his or her respective oral hygiene techniques? What were the bacteria colony counts for each student 60 minutes after using his or her respective oral hygiene techniques? Which oral rinse had the longest-lasting results in reducing the amount of oral bacteria present in the mouths of the students tested at the 30-minute interval? At the 60-minute interval?

PART

III

Appendixes

APPENDIX A

400+ IDEAS FOR SCIENCE FAIR PROJECT TOPICS

The following list of general science fair project subject areas includes various scientific fields and can be used to find a possible project topic. In addition, the websites of government agencies and scholarly associations may supply you with additional information about these subject areas or explain how to obtain a referral to a local mentor in these subject areas. Many of these agencies and associations have sections on their websites specifically geared toward students and some even sponsor special awards at state and regional science fairs.

A

Acoustics
analysis of sound waves
comparison of acoustic models
comparison of materials used for sound amplification
effects on sound dampening
factors affecting sound pitch
methods of noise control
sound holography
study of anechoic chambers
study of the acoustics of music

For information and contacts on this subject, visit Acoustical Society of America at: www.gbcasa.org

Aerodynamics
analysis of, in vehicles
correlation between wheel diameter and speed
drag study
effect of wind design on velocity and distance
effects of turbulence
wind tunnel design

For information and contacts on this subject, visit NASA at: www.grc.nasa.gov/WWW/K-12/airplane/bga.html

Agriculture
analysis of chemicals used in farming
analysis of pesticides used in farming
analysis of various feeds
comparison of soil types
effect of fertilizers on plant and animal life
genetic engineering in agriculture
soil chemistry and composition
study of irrigation methods

For information and contacts on this subject, visit U.S. Department of Agriculture at: www.usda.gov

Air
effects of aerosols
effects of smog
evaluation of air filters
study of airborne infections
study of air quality in various buildings

For information and contacts on this subject, visit National Oceanic and

Atmospheric Administration at: www.arl.noaa.gov

Amino Acids
interaction of, in the body

metabolism of, in the body

method for determining human body absorption rates

Anesthesia
alternative aesthetics

comparison of effects between individuals

side effects of

For information and contacts on this subject, visit American Society of Anesthesiologists at: www.asahq.org

Animals
behavior modification in

communication between

environmental effects on animal behavior

environmental effects on animal migration

genetics and animal breeding

learning in/training of

territoriality in various species

treatment of animal diseases

For information and contacts on this subject, visit American Society for the Prevention of Cruelty to Animals at: www.aspca.org

Antibiotics
analysis of allergic reactions to

comparison of effectiveness between types

sources of

study of bacteria resistance to

For information and contacts on this subject, visit American Medical Association at: www.ama-assn.org

Aquaculture
effects of water temperature and salinity levels on fish hatching

scientific techniques for fisheries

study of algae cultures

study of watershed management standards

use of antimicrobial agents in

For information and contacts on this subject, visit National Aquaculture Association at: www.natlaquaculture.org

Arteries
calcification of

methods for improving arterial circulation

prevention of disease in

study of angiogenesis in

For information and contacts on this subject, visit American Heart Association at: www.americanheart.org

Astronomy
analysis of satellite designs

analysis of telescope designs

effects of cosmic magnetic fields

effects of sunspots on weather systems

predicting the positioning of an object in orbit

study of Doppler imaging of stars

study of the moon's effects on nature

For information and contacts on this subject, visit American Astronomical Society at: www.aas.org

Automobiles
analysis of safety devices for

identification and effects of vehicle emissions

modifications of and improvements in

B

Batteries
comparison of battery types

effects of storage temperatures on

methods for running AC devices on DC power

modifications or improvements in battery chargers

Behavior
behavior modification of children through reinforcement techniques

correlation between handwriting and personality type

correlation between IQ and memory

effects of birth order on social development

effects of classical music on learning

effects of television on social development of children

study of memory retention

For information and contacts on this subject, visit American Psychiatric Association at: www.psych.org

Blood

chemistry and composition of

diseases of

effects on platelet aggregation

effects on the clotting of

regeneration of bone marrow

variations in blood cell counts

For information and contacts on this subject, visit American Association of Blood Banks at: www.aabb.org

Bones

abnormalities in

absorption of calcium supplements by

analysis of fracture types

chemistry and composition of

diseases of

For information and contacts on this subject, visit National Institutes of Health at: www.osteo.org

Botany

biochemical changes in plants in various environments

effects of hormones on plant tissue cultures

effects of soil erosion on plants

external effects on plant growth

medicinal uses of plants

methods for treating crown gall disease

nutrient deficiencies in hydroponically grown plants

plant breeding and crossbreeding analysis

plant cloning techniques

For information and contacts on this subject, visit American Society for Horticulture Science at: www.ashs.org

Brain

abnormalities in

correlation between memory and nucleic acid

diseases of

effects of neurological diagnostic testing

effects of physical injury on

stem cell/spinal cell study

For information and contacts on this subject, visit American Neurological Association at: www.aneuroa.org

Building and Construction

bridge engineering

comparison of insulation materials

comparison of strengths of building materials

effects of earthquakes on structures

effects of weather upon structures

fire preventative building materials

study of strains and stresses

For information and contacts on this subject, visit American Society of Civil Engineers at: www.asce.org

C

Carbohydrates

amounts needed in diet

effects on blood glucose levels

metabolism of

Cellular Phones/Wireless Technology

industrial applications of wireless technology

physiological effects on nonionizing radiation

study of cell phone usage and effect on driving ability

Chemistry

comparison of chemical bonds

effects of chemical reactions

effects of chemical toxins in the environment

effects on crystal growth

methods for absorbing wastewater metallic ions

use of atomic absorption spectroscopy

For information and contacts on this subject, visit American Chemical Society at: www.chemistry.org

Children

learning disorders in

methods for modifying behavior

sleeping needs of

study of childhood diseases

study of growth and development in children

Cigarettes

collection efficiency of cigarette filters

methods to assist others to stop smoking

physiological effects of firsthand smoke compared to secondhand smoke

For information and contacts on this subject, visit American Lung Association at: www.lungusa.org/tobacco

Color

color chromatography in various substances

effects of, on plant growth

perception of

psychological effects of

physiological effects of

Computers

developing various algorithms and code for

program designs for

robotic applications for

Corrosion

methods for the prevention of

role of microbes in

study of chemical changes in

For information and contacts on this subject, visit National Metalizing Association at: www.emetalizing.com

Crystals

applications of chemical crystallography

comparison of structures between various types

factors affecting the growth of

magnetic properties of

mathematical patterns found in

For information and contacts on this subject, visit American Crystallographic Association at: www.hwi.buffalo.edu/ACA

D

Dairy Studies

comparison of animal feeds

effects of dairy products on digestion

effects of hormone additive diets in cows

microbial action in dairy products

natural methods for preserving dairy products

treatment of viruses in dairy cattle

For information and contacts on this subject, visit American Dairy Science Association at: www.adsa.org

E

Environmental Studies

analysis of a closed ecological system or biosphere

analysis of biodegradable substances

effects of pollutants on wildlife

handling and transportation of toxic wastes

landfills and groundwater contamination

neutralization of toxic wastes

study of soil or water purification systems

For information and contacts on this subject, visit Environmental Protection Agency at: www.epa.gov

Erosion

effects of soil composition

effects of weather in

methods for controlling

For information and contacts on this subject, visit National Soil Erosion Research Laboratory at: www.topsoil. nserl.purdue.edu

Eye

color and light sensitivity of

effects of age on peripheral vision

effects of laser surgery upon

effects of ultraviolet radiation on

effects of various vitamin supplements

perception of optical illusions among age groups

study of abnormalities in

study of diseases in

For information and contacts on this subject, visit American Academy of Ophthalmology at: www.aao.org

F

Fermentation

analysis of enzymatic stimulation

applications of yeast in

identification and role of microbes in

study of chemical changes in

For information and contacts on this subject, visit American Society of Brewing Chemists at: www.asbcnet.org

Fertilizers

chemistry and composition of

comparison and evaluation of various types

comparison of organic and inorganic types

effects on the environment

For information and contacts on this subject, visit International Fertilizer Industry Association at: www.fertilizer.org

Fish

comparison of different species

effects of contaminated water on

medicinal uses of fish oils

migration patterns of

study of diseases found in

For information and contacts on this subject, visit American Society of Ichthyologists and Herpetologists at: http://199.245.200.110

Food

allergic reactions to

analysis and comparison of radiated food quality

body absorption of nutrients from

comparison of nutritional contents of

dehydration and preservation of

effects of packing on

effects of pesticides on food quality

food-dwelling microbes

methods of treating contamination of

physiological effects of additives used for preservation

For information and contacts on this subject, visit American Society of Agricultural Engineers at: www.asae.org

Fungi

environmental effects of mold spores

means for preventing the growth of

medicinal uses of

practical applications of for industry

G

Gasoline

analysis of the by-products from

chemistry and composition of

comparison of efficiency of various octane levels

For information and contacts on this subject, visit U.S. Department of Energy at: www.energy.gov

Genetics

genetic mapping in bacteria

methods for transferring genes

studies in plant cloning

study of genetic diseases

Geology

relationship between the moon and earthquake activity

study of earthquake activity

study of flood management and containment

study of the geologic history of an area

study of volcanic activity

For information and contacts on this subject, visit U.S. Geological Survey at: www.usgs.gov/index.html

Gerontology

correlation between mental activity and health in elders

effects on Alzheimer's disease

study of changes in the senses of the elderly

For information and contacts on this
subject, visit American Geriatrics Society
at: www.americangeriatrics.org

Glucose

metabolism in the body

study of sugar inversion

study of treatment of diabetes

For information and contacts on this
subject, visit American Diabetes
Association at: www.diabetes.org

H

Hair

effects of diet on

effects of disease on

hair transplanting techniques

physiological effects of hair dyes and
chemicals

Health

analysis of various diets

analysis of various exercise programs

correlation between pH levels in hair
products and hair quality

effects of climate on

side effects of medications

study of diseases and prevention thereof

For information and contacts on this
subject, visit U.S. Department of Health
and Human Services at: www.os.dhhs.gov

Heart

abnormalities in

effects of diet on

external effects on blood pressure and
pulse rate

study of diseases found in

For information and contacts on this
subject, visit American Heart Association
at: www.americanheart.org

Heat

analysis of efficiency of various heating
mechanisms

chemical reactions that produce heat

effects on chemical changes

insulation for retaining heat

therapeutic uses of

Hydraulics

analysis of turbines

methods for irrigation improvement

pumping design modifications

I

Ice

comparison of various ice melters

effects of, on bodily tissues

effects of, on microbes

therapeutic and surgical uses of

Immune System

in vitro immunization of cells

methods of vaccination

study of biochemical processes in

study of disorders affecting

For information and contacts on this
subject, visit American Autoimmune
Related Diseases Association at:
www.aarda.org/index.html

Infants

chemistry and content of baby
food/formula

presence of hand dexterity and
preference in

study of growth and behavior of

Infrared Rays

effects of, on the environment

effects of, on heating

image converters

industrial applications of

therapeutic uses of

Insects

comparison of species in different
locations

effects of diseases carried by

methods for extermination of

methods for sterilization of

parasitic effects of

study of behavior and communication in

For information and contacts on this
subject, visit Entomological Society of
America at: www.entsoc.org

L

Lasers
applications of lasers and optics
effects of, on the environment
uses of, in communications
uses of, in surgery

Learning
effects of diet on
effects of music on
memory, reasoning, and spatial abilities
  between age groups and gender types
methods for subliminal learning
study of learning disabilities
study of relationship between exercise
  and learning ability

Light
applications of, in photography
influence of, in chemical reactions
psychological effects of
therapeutic uses of

Lipids
amounts needed in diet
analysis of cholesterol tests
metabolism of

Liquids
comparison of surface tension between
  various liquids
effects of, on acoustics
viscosity comparisons

Lungs
effects of nutrition on
environmental effects on
study of diseases found in

For information and contacts on this
subject, visit American Lung Association
at: www.lungusa.org

M

Magnetics
effects of magnetic fields
industrial applications of magnets
medical uses of magnets

For information and contacts on this
subject, visit International Magnetics
Association at: www.intl-magnetics.org

Mathematics
analysis of various functions
correlation between number systems
mathematical patterning in music
mathematical patterning in nature
studies in probability

For information and contacts on this
subject, visit American Mathematical
Society at: www.ams.org

Metabolism
chemical factors affecting
effects of dieting on
effects of diet pills on
variation of, among animals

For information and contacts on this
subject, visit American Association of
Clinical Endocrinology at: www.aace.com

Metals
corrosion inhibitors
oxidation rate comparisons
refining processes
variations in the atomic densities of

For information and contacts on this
subject, visit National Metalizing
Association at: www.emetalizing.com

Meteorology
analysis of weather patterns
artificial effects upon weather
comparison of rainfall between locations
methods for forecasting

For information and contacts on this
subject, visit American Meteorological
Association at: www.ametsoc.org/AMS

Minerals
contents found in various soil samples
contents found in various water samples
medicinal uses of
as nutritional supplements

For information and contacts on this
subject, visit American Mineralogical
Society at: www.minsocam.org

Music
comparing sound quality between digital and analog recording

effects of music on learning

study of differences in tone quality between types of instruments

O

Ocean
effects of pollution on

methods for biodegrading oil spills

ocean waves as an energy source

For information and contacts on this subject, visit National Oceanic and Atmospheric Administration at: www.oar.noaa.gov

Oil
effects of, on the environment

methods for improving underwater drilling oil risers

nontraditional applications in industry

reclamation and recycling of oil

refining modifications

For information and contacts on this subject, visit American Petroleum Institute at: www.api-ec.api.org

Orthopedics
artificial joint designs

prosthetic device designs

study of therapeutic exercises

For information and contacts on this subject, visit American Academy of Orthopaedic Surgeons at: www.aaos.org

P

Parasites
methods for extermination of

prevention of parasitic microbes

study of parasitic diseases

For information and contacts on this subject, visit American Society of Parasitologists at: asp.unl.edu

Pesticides
biodegradation of

effects of, on health

effects of, on the environment

improving the effectiveness of

storage containers for

For information and contacts on this subject, visit Environmental Protection Agency at: www.epa.gov

Photography
effects of temperature on film

lens modifications

methods of surgical use of

uses of laser photography

Plastics
alternative industrial applications for

effects of, on the environment

effects of radiation on

modification of injection molding processes

recycling methods for

surgical applications of

For information and contacts on this subject, visit American Plastics Council at: www.americanplasticscouncil.org

Pollution
analysis of purification mechanisms

analysis of sewage disposal mechanisms

chemistry and composition of various water and soil samples

methods for controlling

For information and contacts on this subject, visit Environmental Protection Agency at: www.epa.gov

Ponds, Lakes, Rivers
analysis of seasonal changes in, on wildlife

analysis of water quality among locations

chemistry and composition of water samples

comparison of dissolved oxygen rates among locations

current power as an energy source

eutrophication in

methods for water purification

For information and contacts on this subject, visit Ecological Society of America at: www.esa.org

Proteins

lipoprotein patterns in various age groups

metabolism of, in various animals

nutritional importance of

study of protein synthesis

For information and contacts on this subject, visit The Protein Society at: www.faseb.org/protein

R

Radiation

effects of nonionizing radiation

methods of protection against

physiological effects of

uses of, in food preservation

uses of, in sterilization

Radiography/Radiology

industrial applications of

physiological side effects of

uses of, in medicine

For information and contacts on this subject, visit Radiological Society of North America at: www.rsna.org

Radios

comparison of power supplies for

electromagnetic emissions from

methods of eliminating radio interference

methods for improving sound in

radio frequency uses

For information and contacts on this subject, visit American Radio Relay League at: www.arrl.org

Rain/Precipitation

chemistry and composition of raindrops

comparison of rainfall patterns among locations

study of rain erosion

For information and contacts on this subject, visit American Meteorological Society at: www.ametsoc.org/ASM

Recycling

comparison of recycling techniques

effects of, on the internal bonding of paper

methods for recycling various materials

methods of developing a waste management system

For information and contacts on this subject, visit National Recycling Coalition at: www.nrc-recycle.org

S

Salt

antibacterial effects of

environmental effects of

physiological effects of

use in preservation

use of, as a fertilizer

Seawater

chemistry and composition of

effects of environment on

oil spill cleanup solutions

study of corrosion by

study of microbes from various ocean locations

Seeds

effects of radiation on

germination techniques

study of diseases in

Sewage

as an energy resource

chemistry and composition of

methods for the purification of

study of the biodegradation of

use of, as a fertilizer

Skin

effects of medication on

effects of ultraviolet radiation on

methods of protecting and improving quality of

methods of skin grafting

study of diseases found in

For information and contacts on this subject, visit American Academy of Dermatology at: www.aad.org

Sleep

effects of, on behavior

effects of sleep deprivation

influence of, on circadian rhythms

methods to stop snoring

observation of various stages of

physiological needs for in children and adults

study of sleeping disorders

For information and contacts on this subject, visit American Academy of Sleep Medicine at: www.aasmnet.org

Soil

effects of microbes on

chemistry and composition of

methods of conservation of

methods for controlling erosion of

Sun

comparison of solar energy with other sources

evaluation of lotions with various sun protection factors

measure of radiation from, at various locations and times

medicinal effects of

T

Telescopes

factors affecting resolution powers in

modifications of

study of various lenses

use of mathematics in

Tobacco

analysis of substitutes for

chemistry and composition of

diseases caused by

use of, as a fertilizer

U

Ultraviolet Rays

effects of, on plants/animals

therapeutic uses of

use of, for water purification

V

Vaccinations

methods of inoculating

physiological side effects of

serum sources

Vitamins/Nutraceuticals

study of deficiencies of

study of interaction between vitamins and medication

study of metabolism of, in the human body

therapeutic uses of

For information and contacts on this subject, visit American Nutraceutical Association at: www.americanutra.com

W

Water

analysis of water quality between various locations

chemistry and composition of

comparison of pH levels between various locations

effects of pollution on

methods of purification of

study of filtration methods

For information and contacts on this subject, visit American Water Works Association at: www.awwa.org

Wildlife

methods for improving habitats of

methods of conservation of

prevention of disease in

For information and contacts on this subject, visit National Wildlife Federation at: www.nwf.org

Wind

comparison of windmill designs

effects of, on soil erosion

study of wind turbines

use of, as an energy source

wind tunnel study

For information and contacts on this subject, visit American Wind Energy Association at: www.awea.org

Wood

chemistry and composition of various types

fireproofing techniques

APPENDIX B

100+ PROJECT TITLES OF AWARD-WINNING PROJECTS

The following is a list of over one hundred actual science fair project titles taken from award-winning science fair projects at a variety of recent state and regional Intel ISEF–affiliated science fairs that may help generate some ideas for you. The topics are broken down by Intel ISEF categories of scientific discipline.

Behavioral and Social Science

Does Hearing a Type of Unfamiliar Music Frequently Increase One's Like or Dislike for It?

Does Color Affect the Way One Feels?

Does Subliminal Imaging Affect Decision Making?

Can Animals Instinctively Select Foods That Are Most Nutritionally Beneficial to Them through the Use of Their Senses?

Does Stress through Physical Exercise Affect One's Cognitive Ability?

Does Right or Left Handedness Affect Overall Lateral Dominance?

Do Behavioral Patterns of Smokers Affect Their Ability to Quit Smoking?

What Is the Best Time of Day for Students of Different Ages to Study?

Does One's Perception of Elapsed Time Vary When They Are Working versus Not Working?

Does a Correlation Exist between Sensory Arousal and the Mozart Effect?

The Relationship between Obsessive-Compulsive Disorder and Birth Order

Biochemistry

The Effects of Glucose on Cell Volume

Does the Percentage of Reduced Fat in Food Correspond to the Same Percentage Change in Calories?

Which Brand of Plastic Zipper Bags Keeps Bread Fresher Longer?

What Are the Effects of Various Cooking Methods on the Depletion of Vitamin C?

A Comparison of the Durability of Latent Fingerprints using Cyanoacrylate and Nonpreserved Latent Fingerprints

Can Calorie Restriction Enhance the Ability of Cells to Survive DNA-Damaging UV Light Exposure?

The Effects of Various Preservatives on the Spoilage of Milk

The Effect of Antacids on E. Coli Found in Hamburger Meat in the Presence of Gastric Fluid

Botany

Plant Growth under Different Wavelengths of Light

Which Plant Food Works the Best?

The Effect of Water Temperature on Various Species of Phytoplankton

The Effects of the Use of Antagonistic Microorganisms in Controlling Fruit Rot

If Music Affects Plant Growth, What Type of Music Has the Most Impact?

Does Altering the Gravity of Bean Plants Affect Their Growth?

Does the Increase of Oxygen Concentration Enhance the Germination Rate of Plant Seeds?

Does Water Type Affect the Height of Grass?

The Effects of Mature Leaf Position on Stomatal Development in New Leaves in Response to Carbon Dioxide Levels

How Does Radiation Affect the Growth and Germination of Radish Seeds?

What Type of Animal Manure Will Have the Most Positive Growth Effect on Plants?

Can Wheat Gluten Be Used as a Natural Preemergent Herbicide Like Corn Gluten Meal?

Which Filamentous Algae Can Recycle Carbon Dioxide into Oxygen Most Efficently?

Which Variable, Namely, Species Type, Tree Size, or Seed Mass Has the Most Effect on the Ability of a Maple Tree to Reproduce?

Chemistry

Does Prewatering Soil Significantly Reduce Runoff during Normal Rainfall?

Does pH in the Intestine Affect the Absorption of Calcium in the Body?

Does Temperature Affect Battery Life?

The Effects of Light Intensity and Temperature on the Rate of the Photochemical Reaction of Silver Chloride

Does the Electrolytic Rates of Different Beverages Affect the Rate at Which the Body Receives Energy from the Beverage?

The Effect of Temperature on Surface Tension Strength

Which Type of Juice Beverage Is the Most Effective Means for Delivering Vitamin C to the Human Body?

Which Papier-maché Adhesive Ingredient Is the Strongest?

Which Brand of Paint Preserves the Tensile Strength of Steel?

How Do Different Solutions Affect the Carbon Dioxide Production of Leavening Agents?

How Do Different Types of Water Affect the Rusting Process of Various Metals?

Does Cooking Acidic Foods in Aluminum Cookware Cause Traces of Aluminum to Leach into the Food?

What Substance Could Be Applied to Pretreat Airplane Wings to Aid in the Rapid Removal of Ice?

A Comparison of the Thermal Transport Properties of Water and Ethylene Glycol

Does Molarity Affect the Amount of Crystals Formed in the Electrolysis of Copper Sulfate, Aluminum Nitrate, and Iron Sulfate?

Does the Introduction of Protein Affect the Growth of the Crystalline Structural Lattice in Sodium Chloride?

Computer Science

Optimal Configuration of School Bus Routes Using the Computer Based Algorithm— Simulated Annealing

Can a Computer Learn Game Strategy by Analyzing Results over a Period of Time

Can Enlarged Images Be Depixelized?

Earth and Space Science

Are There Jet Stream Patterns That Affect Tornado Formation and and Location?

The Effect of Gravity on Stress Response in Plants

Analysis of Soil Types for Strength

Effects of Soils and Surfaces on Water Runoff and Flooding

The Effects of Earthquakes on Small Structures

What Is the Structure to Prevent Beach Erosion?

What Shape of a Solar Reflector Reflects the Most Light into a Solar Cell?

The Effects of Fin Configuration on the Performance of a Model Rocket

Do Soils Change the Composition of Water?

Engineering

What Is the Best Type of Guardrail for an Inclining Mountain Road

Is It Possible to Give a Prosthetic Limb Device the Ability to Be Felt by the Nerves of a Patient

Testing the Efficacy of Chest Protectors from Ball or Hockey Puck Impact

Can a Temporary Wheelchair Lift Be Constructed That Will Not Obstruct Stairs or Require Modifications to Exisitng Staircase Structures?

Environmental Science

What Glass Color Blocks Ultraviolet Rays the Best?

The Effects of Soil on Home Insulation

The Effects of Marine Paint on Sea Life

The Effect of Respirable Particles from Radial Tire Wear on Human Lungs

Environmental Effects of Biodegradable Detergents

A Chemical Investigation and Analysis of Ground and Surface Water in a Local Water Supply

The Effect of Water Hardness on Toxicity

Phototoxicity of Botanical Compounds to Insects and Yeast

The Effects of Radon in Water

Effects of Fertilization of Golf Courses on Drinking Water

Does Temperature Affect Solar Cell Performance?

Does the Distance That Water Travels from a Water Plant Affect the Amount of Lead in the Drinking Water?

Can Citrus Oils Be Used As a Substitute for Gasoline?

Are There Adequate Amounts of Carbon and Nitrogen in Soil after a Forest Fire to Affect Plant Growth?

Can Earthworms Decontaminate Soil Contaminated with Lead?

The Effects of Sugar, Coffee Pulp, and Alcohol on the Rate that *Eisenia foetida* Can Decompose Garbage

Gerontology

Does Age Affect One's Sense of Smell or Taste?

The Physiologic Effect of a Vegetarian Diet on the Elderly

The Effects of the Herb *Succus cineraria* Martima on the Size Distribution of Cataract Proteins

Health Science

The Effects of Air Pressure on Blood Clots

Can Antisense Genes Reverse Antibiotic Resistance?

The Long-term Effects of Antibacterial Soap on Normal Skin Flora

What Is the Effect of Varying Levels of pH on *Eschericia coli?*

Which Whitening Agents Whiten Teeth Best?

Do Colored Contact Lenses Affect Peripheral Vision?

How Effective Is Sunscreen Against Ultraviolet Light?

Effect of Light on the Development of Rat Mammary Glands

Does the Addition of Fibroblast Growth Factor (FGF) Retard the Cancerous Growth of Tumors in Rats?

Which Antacid Will Neutralize the Most Stomach Acid?

The Effects of Nicotine on Angiogenesis-related Processes and Its Impact on Tumor Growth

Which Acne-Fighting Agent—Salicylic Acid, Benzoyl Peroxide, or Sulfur—works Best at Eradicating *Staphylococcus epidermis?*

Is There a Direct Relationship between Body Mass Index and Blood Pressure in Teenagers?

Mathematics

The Relationship Between the Golden Ratio and Facial Perception

Is the Distribution of Differences between Prime Numbers Predictable or Chaotic?

Is There a Statistical Advantage to Winning in Baseball for the Team That Scores First in the Game?

Microbiology

The Effect of Ultraviolet Radiation on the Growth of Bacteria on Meat

Can Bacteria Become Resistant to Antibacterial Products Containing Triclosan, an Antibacterial agent?

Do Synthetic or Nonsynthetic Emulsifiers Break Down Fat the Best?

The Effects of Preservatives in Bread and the Rate of Mold Growth

Can an Antibiotic-Resistant Bacteria Be Changed into an Antibiotic-Sensitive Bacteria?

The Effect of Phosphates on the Luminescence of Aerobic Marine Light-Emitting Bacteria

What Are the Effects of Atrazine, an Herbicide, on Bacterial Survival?

Do Biofilms Grow on Contact Lenses?

Can Bacteria Found on the Hands Become Resistant to Antibacterial Liquid Hand Soap?

Physics

Does the Frequency and Amplitude of Sound Waves from a Violin Change in Different Temperatures?

Can Sound Be Transmitted through a Laser Beam?

Does String Tension Affect the Rate at How Quickly a Tennis Racket's Strings Break?

The Effect of Balde Angle and Barometric Pressure on the Rotation Speed of A Windmill

Is there a Difference in Tone Quality Between Plastic and Wooden Clarinets?

How do Sound Waves Behave When Traveling Through Carbon Dioxide?

What Type of Flooring Has the Strongest Sound Vibrations?

Which Type of Shoe Insert Absorbs the Most Shock on Impact?

What is the Relationship Between Barrier Thickness and the Percentage of Light That Tunnels through a Barrier?

What Properties of a Truss Affect its Displacement?

How Does Shape Affect the Drag of an Object?

A Study of Heat Absorption and Dispersion on Various Colors of Metallic Paint

Zoology

The Effects of Citronella Oil, Peppermint Oil and Tea Tree Oil as a Natural Pesticide on the Eradication of Mosquitos

Which Types of Soils do Worms Prefer?

The Effects of Electromagnetic Fields on the Development and Behavior of Caterpillars

Is There a Relationship Between the Number of Days it Takes Fruit Fly Eggs to Hatch and the Amount of Light They are Exposed To?

Does Water Temperature Affect the Hatch Rate of Mosquitoes?

Does the Amount of Light Exposure Affect the Response of Euglena Populations to Acidic Polutants?

APPENDIX C

SCIENTIFIC SUPPLY COMPANIES

The following is a list of over twenty-five scientific supply companies from whom laboratory and other scientific supplies and instruments can be obtained. The companies were selected because they specialize in equipment geared to science fair projects or equipment that is normally used in a school laboratory.

Northeast and Atlantic

Auspex Scientific
1416 Union Boulevard
Allentown, PA 18109
(610) 351-2079
www.auspexscientific.com

Connecticut Valley Biological
   Supply Co.
82 Valley Rd.
P.O. Box 326
Southampton, MA 01703
(413) 527-4030
(800) 628-7748
www.ctvalleybio.com

Edmund Scientific Co.
60 Pearce Ave.
Tonawanda, NY 14150-6711
(800) 728-6999
www.scientificsonline.com

MiniScience.Com
1059 Main Ave.
Clifton, NJ 07011
(973) 777-3133
www.miniscience.com

The Science Fair, Inc.
140 College Square
Newark, DE 19711-5447
(302) 453-1817

(800) 304-9403
www.thesciencefair.com

Science Kit and Boreal Labs
777 E. Park Dr.
P.O. Box 5003
Tonawanda, NY 14150
(800) 828-7777
www.sciencekit.com

Thomas Scientific
P.O. Box 99
Swedesboro, NJ 08085
(856) 467-3087
(800) 345-5232
www.thomassci.com

Ward's Natural Science
P.O. Box 92912
Rochester, NY 14692-9012
(800) 962-2660
www.wardsci.com

Southeast

Advance Scientific & Chemical, Inc.
2345 S.W. 34th St.
Fort Lauderdale, FL 33312
(800) 524-2436
www.advance-scientific.com

Carolina Biological Supply Co.
2700 York Rd.
Burlington, NC 27215
(800) 334-5551
www.carolina.com

Kenin Scientific Discount
1830 N.E. 163 St.
North Miami Beach, FL 33162
(800) 600-6291
www.kenin.com

Science Hobbies, Inc.
901-D North Wendover Road
Charlotte, NC 28211
(704) 367-2215
www.sciencehobbies.net

Midwest

American Science & Surplus
5316 N. Milwaukee Ave.
Chicago, IL
(847) 647-0011
www.sciplus.com

BME Lab Store
2459 University Ave., W.
St. Paul, MN 55114
(651) 646-5339

Fisher Science Education
4500 Turnberry
Hanover Park, IL 60133
(800) 955-1177
www.fisheredu.com

Frey Scientific Co.
100 Paragon Parkway
Manfield, OH 44905
(800) 225-3739
www.freyscientific.com

Sargent-Welch
7300 N. Linden Ave.
P.O. Box 5229
Buffalo Grove, IL 60089-5229
(800) 727-4368
www.sargentwelch.com

South Central

Capitol Scientific, Inc.
2500 Rutland St.
Austin, TX 78766
(512) 836-1167

NASCO
901 Janesville Ave.
Fort Atkinson, WI 53538
(800) 558-9595
www.enasco.com

Sciencelab.com
4338 Haven Glen
Kingwood, TX 77339
(281) 348-9500
www.sciencelab.com

Science Stuff
1104 Newport Ave.
Austin, TX 78753-4019
(800) 795-7315
www.sciencestuff.com

West

All World Scientific
5515 186 Place SW
Lynnwood, WA 98037
425 672 4228
800- 28-WORLD
www.awscientific.com

Amico Scientific
1161 Cushman Ave.
San Diego, CA 92110
(619) 543-9200

A. Warren's Educational Supplies
980 W. San Bernardino Road
Covina, CA 91722
(800) 523-7767
www.warrenseducational.com

Hawaii Chemical & Scientific
2364 North King St.
Honolulu, HI 96811
(808) 841-4265
www.hawaiiscientific.com

Tri-Ess Sciences
1020 Chestnut St.
Burbank, CA 91506
(818) 848-7838
800-274-6910 (outside California)
www.tri-esssciences.com

Canada

Northwest Scientific Supply
P.O. Box 6100 # 301-3060
Cedar Hill Road
VICTORIA, BC
V8T 3J5
CANADA
(250) 592-2438
www.nwscience.com

APPENDIX D

STATE, REGIONAL, AND INTERNATIONAL SCIENCE AND ENGINEERING FAIRS

There are many wonderful science and engineering fairs throughout the United States and around the world. Since many of these fairs change administrators or names yearly, it is impossible to list all of them. Therefore, this list contains the name of state, regional, and international science and engineering fairs that are currently charter affiliated with the Intel International Science and Engineering Fair. These fairs are held annually on various dates from February through May. While these fairs play host to thousands of top science fair exhibits from students in grades 6–12, only students in grades 9–12 from these fairs are eligible to participate in the annual Intel International Science and Engineering Fair, which is administered by Science Service, Inc.

The following is a list of all affiliated fairs and their hosting cities along with their corresponding website addresses, if available. We have listed websites that have been online for awhile so we hope they will still be around by the time you read this. The names, addresses and telephone numbers of fair administrators, as well as the specific dates of these fairs, have not been included because they often change on a yearly basis. However, if you would like to obtain specific information about any of the listed fairs, contact Science Service, Inc., 1719 N. Street, N.W., Washington, D.C. 20036. Telephone (202) 785-2255.

United States

Alabama

Livingston: West Alabama Science and
   Engineering Fair
(205) 652-3414

Alaska

Juneau: Southeast Alaska Regional
   Science Fair
www.asd.k12.ak.us/Depts/Science/
   sciencefair/sciencefair.htm

Arizona

Prescott: Northern Arizona Regional
   Science and Engineering Fair
http://sciencefair.pr.erau.edu

Sierra Vista: SSVEC's Youth
   Engineering and Science Fair
http://ssvec.org/CommunityPrograms/
   yesfair.asp

Tempe: Central Arizona Regional Science
   and Engineering Fair
www.carsef.asu.edu

Tucson: Southern Arizona Regional
Science and Engineering Fair
www.sarsef.com

Arkansas

Batesville: North Central Arkansas
Regional Science Fair
www.lyon.edu

Conway: Arkansas State Science Fair

Fayetteville: Northwest Arkansas
Regional Science Science and
Engineering Fair
www.uark.edu/~k12info

Hot Springs: West Central Regional
Science Fair

Jonesboro: Northeast Arkansas Regional
Science Fair
http://nearsf.astate.edu

Monticello: Southeast Arkansas Regional
Science Fair

California

Carson: South Bay Regional Science &
Engineering Fair

Danville: Tri-Valley Science and
Engineering Fair
http://tvsef.llnl.gov

Sacramento: Sacramento Regional
Science & Engineering Fair
www.srsefair.org

San Diego: Greater San Diego Science
and Engineering Fair
www.gsdsef.org

San Francisco: San Francisco Bay Area
Science Fair, Inc.
http://home.pacbell.net/sfbasf/

San Jose: Synopsys Silicon Valley Science
and Technology Championship
www.science-fair.org

Santa Cruz: Santa Cruz County Science
Fair
www.science.santacruz.k12.ca.us

Seaside: Monterey County Science and
Engineering Fair
www.nps.navy.mil/mcsfp/

Colorado

Alamosa: San Luis Valley Regional
Science Fair, Inc.
http://slv.adams.edu/science/index.htm

Boulder: Boulder Valley Regional Science
Fair

Colorado Springs: Pikes Peak Regional
Science Fair

Denver: The Denver Metro Regional
Science & Engineering Fair
www.uchsc.edu/ahec/sciencefair/
index.htm

Fort Collins: Colorado Science and
Engineering Fair
www.csef.colostate.edu

Grand Junction: Western Colorado
Science Fair

Greeley: Longs Peak Science and
Engineering Fair
http://hopper.unco.edu/Other/
Sciencefair.html

La Junta: Arkansas Valley Regional
Science Fair

San Juan Basin Regional Science Fair
http://faculty.fortlewis.edu/
IVERSON_M/sciencefair.htm

Sterling: Northeast Colorado Regional
Science Fair

Connecticut

Hamden: Connecticut State Science Fair
http://ctsciencefair.org

New Milford: Science Horizons Science
Fair & Symposium
www.sciencehorizons.org

Florida

Arcadia: Heartland Regional Science and
Engineering Fair

Bradenton: Manatee Regional Science
and Engineering Fair

Bushnell: Sumter County Regional
Science Fair

Crystal River: Citrus Regional Science
and Engineering Fair

Fort Myers: Thomas Alva Edison East
Regional Science Fair

Fort Pierce: Treasure Coast Regional
Science and Engineering Fair

Kissimmee: The Osceola Regional
Science Fair

Melbourne: South Brevard Science and
Engineering Fair

Merritt Island: Brevard Intracoastal
Regional Science and Engineering
Fair

Miami: South Florida Science and
Egineering Fair
http://mathscience.dadeschools.net/
sciencefair.htm

Ocala: Big Springs Regional Science Fair

Orange Park: Clay Kiwanis Science Fair

Panama City: Florida Three Rivers
Regional Science and Engineering
Fair

Pinellas Park: Pinellas Regional Science
and Engineering Fair

Sanford: Seminole County Regional
Science, Mathematics & Engineering
Fair

Sarasota: Sarasota Regional Science,
Engineering and Technology Fair
www.sarasota.k12.fl.us/brookside/aoft/
at6/science/science%5Ffair.htm

Titusville: Brevard Mainland Regional
Science and Engineering Fair

Wesley Chapel: PASCO Regional Science
and Engineering Fair

West Palm Beach: Palm Beach County
Science and Engineering Fair

Georgia

Albany: Darton College/Merck Regional
Science Fair

Athens: Georgia State Science and
Engineering Fair
www.uga.edu/oasp/gsef/gsef.html

Atlanta: Atlanta Science and Mathematics
Congress
http://1sblackburn@atlantak12.ga.us

Atlanta: The Earthlink Dekalb-Rockdale
Science & Engineering Fair

Augusta: CSRA Regional Science &
Engineering Fair
http://csrascience.org

Brunswick: Coastal Georgia Regional
Science and Engineering Fair

Savannah: Savannah Ogeechee
Regional Science and Engineering
Fair

Warner Robins: Houston Regional
Science and Engineering Fair

Hawaii

Honolulu: Hawaii State Science and
Engineering Fair
www.hawaii.edu/acadsci

Kahului: Maui Schools Science and
Technology Fair

Kapaa: Kauai Regional Science &
Engineering Fair

Pearl City: Leeward District High School
Science Fair

Illinois

Macomb: Heart of Illinois Science and
Engineering Fair

Indiana

Angola: Northeastern Indiana Tri-State
Regional Science Fair

Evansville: Tri-State Regional Science and
Engineering Fair

Fort Wayne: Northeastern Indiana
Reginal Science and Engineering
Fair
http://ipfw.edu/scifair

Muncie: East Central Indiana Regional
Science Fair

South Bend: Northern Indiana Regional
Science and Engineering Fair

Westville: Northwestern Indiana Science
and Engineering Fair
www.purduenc.edu/cd/scifair.index.html

Iowa

Ames: State Science and Engineering
Fair of Iowa
www.public.iastate.edu/~isstf/

Cedar Rapids: Eastern Iowa Science and
Engineering Fair
www.eisef.org

Indianola: South Central Iowa Science
and Engineering Fair

Kansas

Overland Park: Greater Kansas City
Science and Engineering Fair
http://spioneers.com

Kentucky

Bowling Green: Southern Kentucky
Regional Science Fair

Owensboro: Owensboro-Western
Kentucky Regional Fair

Louisiana

Baton Rouge: Louisiana Science and
Engineering Fair
www.doce.lsu.edu/lsef/

Houma: Terrebonne Parish Science Fair

Lafayette: Louisiana Region VI Science
and Engineering Fair

Lake Charles: Louisiana Region V
Science and Engineering Fair
www.lasciencefair.org

Thibodaux: Louisiana Region X Science
and Engineering Fair

Maryland

Baltimore: Morgan State University

Science-Mathematics-Engineering Fair

Frederick: Frederick County Science
and Engineering Fair

Gaithersburg: Mongomery Area Science
Fair

Laplata: Charles County Science Fair

Largo: Prince George's Area Science
Fair
http://users.erols.com/gorthome/
hpsfmain.htm

Massachusetts

Amherst: Massachusetts Region I
Science Fair
www.scifair.com

Boston: Massachusetts Region VI
Science Fair
www.scifair.com

Bridgewater: Massachusetts Region V
Science Fair
www.scifair.com

Cambridge: Massachusetts State
Science Fair
www.scifair.com

Fall River: Massachusetts Region III
Science Fair
www.scifair.com

Somerville: Massachusetts Region IV
Science Fair
www.scifair.com

Worcester: Massachusetts Region II
State Science Fair
www.scifair.com

Michigan

Ann Arbor: Southeast Michigan Science
Fair

Detroit: Science and Engineering Fair of
Metropolitan Detroit
www.sefmd.org

Flint: Flint Area Science Fair
www.flintsciencefair.org

Port Huron: St. Clair County Science and
Engineering Fair

Minnesota

Duluth: Northeast Minnesota Regional
Science Fair
www.css.edu/USERS/lmcgahey/
web/RegionalSF/main.html

Mankato: South Central/South
Minnesota Regional Science and
Engineering Fair
www.mnsu.edu/sciencefair

Minneapolis: Minnesota Academy of
Science State Fair
www.mnacadsci.org

Minneapolis: Twin Cities Regional
Science Fair
www.tcrsf.org

Moorhead: Western Minnesota Regional
Science Fair

Rochester: Rochester Regional Science
Fair

Saint Cloud: Central Minnesota Regional
Science Fair and Research paper
Program

Winona: Southeast Minnesota Regional
Science Fair

Mississippi

Booneville: Mississippi Region IV
Science Fair

Greenville: Mississippi Region III
Science and Engineering
Fair

Hattiesburg: University of Southern
Mississippi Region I Science and
Engineering Fair

Oxford: Mississippi VII Science and
Engineering Fair
www.outreach.olemiss.edu/youth/
science_fair.html

Missouri

Cape Girardeau: Southeast Missouri
Regional Science Fair
www2.semo.edu/scifair/general.pdf

Jefferson City: Lincoln University
Regional Science Fair

Joplin: Missouri Southern Regional
Science Fair
www.mssc.edu/isef

Saint Joseph: Mid-America Regional
Science and Engineering Fair

Springfield: Ozarks Science and
Engineering Fair
www.k12science.smsu.edu

St. Peters: St. Charles-Lincoln Country
Regional Science and Engineering
Fair

Montana

Billings: Deaconess Billings Clinic
Research Division Science Expo
http://billingsclinic.com/Research/
ScienceExpo.htm

Butte: Southwest Montana Regional
Science and Engineering Fair
http://mtech.edu/outreach/
sciencefair.htm

Missoula: Montana Science Fair
http://hawk.cs.umt.edu/scifair

Nebraska

Greater Nebraska Science and
Engineering Fair
www.gnsef.org

Nevada

Elko: Elko County Science Fair

Reno: Western Nevada Regional Science
and Engineering Fair

New Jersey

Lawrenceville: Mercer Science and
Engineering Fair

North Branch: North Jersey Regional
Science Fair
http://njrsf.org

New Mexico

Albuquerque: Northwestern New
Mexico Regional Science and
Engineering Fair
www.unm.edu/~scifair

Albuquerque: National American Indian
Science and Engineering Fair
www.aises.org

Farmington: San Juan New Mexico
Regional Science and Engineering
Fair

Las Cruces: Southwestern New Mexico
Regional Science and Engineering
Fair
www.nmsu.edu/~scifair/

Las Vegas: Northeastern New Mexico
Regional Science and Engineering
Fair
www.nmhu.edu/sciencefair/

New York

Brooklyn: Polytechnic University and NYC Board of Education Math, Science, and Technology Fair

Long Island: Long Island Science and Engineering Fair
www.lisef.org

Plainview: New York State Science & Engineering Fair
www.NYSSEF.org

Poughkeepsie: Dutchess County Regional Science Fair

Rochester: Central Western Section— Science Teachers Association of NY State Science Congress

Syracuse: Greater Syracuse Scholastic Science Fair
http://most.org/p_gsssf_main.cfm

Troy: Greater Capital Region Science and Engineering Fair

Utica: Utica College Regional Science Fair

Westchester: Progenics Westchester Science and Engineering Fair
www.wesef.org

North Dakota

Dickinson: Southwest North Dakota Regional Science and Engineering Fair

Fargo: Southeast North Dakota Regional Science and Engineering Fair

Grand Forks: Northeast North Dakota Regional Science and Engineering Fair

Jamestown: Southeast Central North Dakota Science and Engineering Fair

Minot: Northwest Central North Dakota Regional Science Fair

Watford City: Northwest North Dakota Regional Science Fair

Ohio

Alliance: Ohio Region XIII Science and Engineering Fair

Archbold: Northwest Ohio Science and Engineering Fair

Athens: Southeastern Ohio Regional Science and Engineering Fair
www.ohiou.edu/scifair/

Cleveland: Northeastern Ohio Science and Engineering Fair
neohioscifair.org

Columbus: Buckeye Science and Engineering Fair
www.ohiosci.org

Marion: Marion Area Science and Engineering Fair

Shaker Heights: Hathaway Brown Upper School

Wilberforce: Miami Valley Science and Engineering Fair

Oklahoma

Ada: Oklahoma State Science and Engineering Fair
http://ecok.edu/ossef

Alva: Northwestern Oklahoma State University Regional Science Fair

Edmond: Central Oklahoma Regional Science and Engineering Fair
http://science.ucok.edu/science-fair.html

Miami: Northeastern Oklahoma A&M Science and Engineering Fair
www.neoam.cc.ok.us/sef

Muskogee: Muskogee Regional Science and Engineering Fair

Oklahoma City: Oklahoma City Regional Science and Engineering Fair

Seminole: East Central Oklahoma Regional Science and Engineering Fair

Tulsa: Tulsa Regional Science and Engineering Fair

Wilburton: Eastern Oklahoma Regional Science and Engineering Fair

Oregon

Beaverton: Beaverton School District Science Expo

Coos Bay: Southwestern Oregon Regional Science Exposition

Portland: Intel Northwest Science Expo
www.cse.pdx.edu/nwse

West Linn: CREST- Jane Goodall Science Symposium

Pennsylvania

Carlisle: The Patriot-News Capital Area Science and Engineering Fair

Lancaster: Lancaster Newspapers Science and Engineering Fair
www.lancasteronline.com/nie/scifair.shtm

Philadelphia: Delaware Valley Science Fair
www.dvsf.org

Pittsburgh: Pittsburgh Regional Science and Engineering Fair
www.pittsburghsciencefair.org

Reading: Reading and Berks Science and Engineering Fair

Rhode Island

Warwick: Rhode Island Science and Engineering Fair

South Carolina

Aiken: Central Savannah River Area Science and Engineering Fair
www.csrascience.org

Charleston: Lowcountry Science Fair

Clemson: Anderson-Oconee-Pickens Regional Science Fair
www.ces.clemson.edu/aophub/sciencefair

Columbia: USC Central South Carolina Region II Science and Engineering Fair

Greensville: Greensville County & South Regional 1A Science and Engineering Fair

Spartanburg: Piedmont South Carolina Region III Science Fair

South Dakota

Aberdeen: Northern South Dakota Science and Math Fair

Brookings: Eastern South Dakota Science and Engineering Fair
ww3.sdstate.edu/Academics/ScienceandEngineeringFair/Index.cfm

Isabel: Northwest Area Schools Regional Science and Engineering Fair

Mitchell: South Central South Dakota Science and Engineering Fair
www.dwusciencefair.com

Rapid City: High Plains Regional Science and Engineering Fair
www.hpcnet.org/science

Tennessee

Chattanooga: Chattanooga Regional Science and Engineering Fair

Cookeville: Cumberland Plateau Regional Science and Engineering Fair
www.tntech.edu/physics

Knoxville: Southern Appalachian Science and Engineering Fair
www.acad.utk.edu/sasef

Memphis: Memphis-Shelby County Science and Engineering Fair

Nashville: Middle Tennessee Science and Engineering Fair
www.vuse.vanderbilt.edu/~scifair/intro.html

Texas

Arlington: Exxon Mobil Texas Science and Engineering Fair
science.uta.edu/emtsef

Austin: Austin Area Science Festival
www.sciencefest.austinenergy.com

Brownsville: Rio Grande Valley Regional Science and Engineering Fair

College Station: Brazos Valley Regional Science and Engineering Fair
http://outreach.science.tamu.edu

Dallas: Dallas Morning News—Toyota Reg. Science and Engineering Fair
http://DallasScienceFair.org

El Paso: Sun Country Science Fair

Forth Worth: Forth Worth Regional Science Fair
www.fwrsf.org

Houston: Science Engineering Fair of Houston
http://uhd.edu/naturalscience

Kilgore: East Texas Regional Science Fair

Laredo: United Independent School District Regional Science Fair
www.uisd.net

San Angelo: District XI Texas Science Fair

San Antonio: Alamo Regional Science and Engineering Fair

Waco: Central Texas Science and Engineering Fair
http://ctsef.org

Utah

Cedar City: Utah Science and Engineering Fair

Ogden: Ogden Area I Science and Engineering Fair

Ogden: Harold W. & Helen M. Ritchey State Science and Engineering Fair of Utah

Provo: Central Utah Science and Engineering Fair
www.cusef.byu.edu

Salt Lake City: Salt Lake City Valley Regional Science & Engineering Fair
www.utah.edu/uees/fair

Virginia

Arlington: Northern Virginia Science and Engineering Fair

Ashburn: Loudoun County Regional Science and Engineering Fair

Ashland: Virginia State Science and Engineering Fair

Charlottesville: Piedmont Regional Science Fair

Dublin: Blue Ridge Highlands Regional Science Fair

Fairfax: Fairfax County Regional Science and Engineering Fair
www.fcps.edu/dis/sciengfair

Harrisonburg: Shenandoah Valley Regional Science Fair

Lynchburg: Central Virginia Regional Science Fair

www.cvgs.k12.va.us/scifair

Manassas: Prince William-Manassas Regional Science Fair

Roanoke: Western Virginia Regional Science Fair

Suffolk: Tidewater Science Fair
www.sps.k12.va.us

Washington

Kennwick: Mid-Columbia Regional Science and Engineering Fair
www.mcsf.net

Tacoma: South Sound Regional Science Fair
www.plu.edu/~scifair

West Virginia

Huntington: West Virginia State Science and Engineering Fair
www.wvssef.org

Keyser: West Virginia Eastern Panhandle Regional High School Science Fair

Montgomery: Central and Southern West Virginia Regional Science and Engineering Fair
www.wvutech.edu/sciencefair

Wisconsin

Glendale: Nicolet Science and Engineering Fair

Milwaukee: USM—Science Fair

Wyoming

Greybull: Northern Wyoming District Science Fair

Outside the United States
American Samoa

Pago Pago: American Samoa Science Fair

Australia

Sydney: Intel Young Scientist Awards
www.stansw.asn.au

Belarus

Minsk: BelJunior
www.unibel.by

Brazil

Novo Hamburgo: National Science and
  Technology Fair
http://liberato.com.br

San Paulo: Febrace – Feira Brasileira de
  Ciencias E Engenharia-Regional Sao
  Paulo

Canada

Hamilton, Ontario: Bay Area Science and
  Engineering Fair
http://basef.mcmaster.ca

Montreal, Quebec: Montreal Regional
  SciTech Fair
www.eascitech.org

China

Beijing: Children Science Fair of Beijing

Beijing: CASTIC (China Adolescents and
  Technology Invention Contest)

Fuzhou City: CASTIC (China
  Adolescents and Technology
  Invention Contest)

Hefei City: CASTIC (China Adolescents
  and Technology Invention Contest)

Hong Kong: Hong Kong Youth Science
  and Technology Invention Contest
www.newgen.org.hk

Shanghai: CASTIC (China Adolescents
  and Technology Invention Contest)

Shanghai: The Children Science Fair of
  Shanghai

Czech Republic

Holesov: Students' Professional
  Activities (SPA)

Denmark

Copenhagen: Unge Forskere

Germany

Stuttgart and Jena
www.jugend-forscht.de

Hungary

Budapest: Innovation Contest for Young
  Scientists
www.innovacio.hu

India

Mumbai: Intel Science Talent Discovery
  Fair—West

New Delhi: Intel Science Talent
  Discovery Fair—North

Ireland

Dublin: EAST BT Young Scientist &
  Technology Exhibition
www.esatbtyoungscientist.com

Israel

Jerusalem: Young Scientists in Israel—
  Contest
www.mada.org.il

Italy

Milano: Giovani E Le Scienze
www.fast.mi.it

Japan

Tokyo: Japan Students Science Awards

Kazakhsta

Astana: DARYN National Junior Science
  Projects Competition

Northern Ireland

Belfast: Seagate Young Innovators

Norway

Oslo: Norwegian Contest for Young
  Scientists
www.unge-forskere.no/stiftelsen

Philippines

Manila: Intel Basic Philippine Science
  Fair

Manila: Intel Philippine Applied Science
  Fair

Portugal

Porto: Portuguese Contest for Young Scientists
www.fjuventude.pt

Puerto Rico

Arecibo: Arecibo Regional Science Fair

Bayamon: Bayamon Regional Science Fair

Caguas: Caguas Regional Science Fair

Cayey: Radians Science & Engineering Fair

Fajardo: Fajardo Regional Science Fair

Guaynabo: San Juan Archdiocesan Regional Science Fair

Gurabo: Humacao Regional Science Fair

Manati: Morovis Regional Science Fair

Mayaguez: Mayaguez Regional Science Fair

Ponce: Ponce Regional Science Fair

San German: San German Regional Scinece Fair

San Juan: Regional Mathematics Fair

San Juan: San Juan Regional Science Fair

Russia

Lipetsk: Russian Youth Program "Step into the Future"

Moscow: Russian Youth Program "Step into the Future"
www.apfn.bmstu.ru

Moscow: Intel-Avangard
www.1303.ru

Murmansk: Russian Youth Program "Step into the Future"

Snezhinsk: Russian Youth Program "Step into the Future"

Usolye-Sibirskoye: Russian Youth Program "Step into the Future"
www.shag-irkutsk.nm.ru

South Africa

Pretoria: Expo for Young Scientists— South Africa
www.exposcience.co.za

South Korea

Seoul: Korea Olympiad in Informatics

Sweden

Stockholm: Utstallningen Unga Forskare
www.fuf.org

Taiwan

Taipei: National Science and Engineering Fair of Republic of China
www.ntsec.gov.tw

Thailand

Bangkok: National Science Projects Competition
www.scisoc.or.th

United Kingdom

London: The BA Science Fair
www.the-ba.net

Virgin Islands

St. Croix: Good Hope School Science Fair

APPENDIX E

ALTERNATIVE SCIENCE FAIR PROJECT COMPETITIONS

This book emphasizes the preparation of science projects for traditional science fair competitions. These fairs are usually state and regional competitions affiliated with the Intel International Science and Engineering Fair. Some students preparing projects for these fairs may qualify to enter their work in other science competitions as well.

While there are numerous alternative science programs and competitions, this section covers the four largest: the Intel Science Talent Search, the Siemens Competition, the National Junior Science and Humanities Symposium, and the Discovery Channel Young Scientist Challenge.

Intel Science Talent Search

This is considered one of the oldest and most prestigious science competitions in the United States. Like the Intel International Science and Engineering Fair and the Discovery Channel Young Scientist Challenge, this competition is administered through Science Service. Several past alumni of the Science Talent Search have become Nobel laureates in physics and chemistry, recipients of the Fields Medal in Mathematics, the National Medal of Science, and many other prestigious awards and distinctions.

From nearly 2,000 completed entry forms and application materials received every year, 300 semifinalists are initially selected who, along with their schools, receive a matching cash award. Then, from this group of 300 semifinalists, 40 finalists are selected to attend the National Academy of Sciences for the Science Talent Institute in Washington, D.C. to exhibit their research and compete for the grand prize of a four-year $100,000 scholarship. In addition to the grand prize there are substantial scholarships for students in second through tenth place, and the remaining 30 finalists are guaranteed a minimum scholarship of $5,000. First-through tenth-place scholarships are disbursed in eight equal installments to the college at which the winning students matriculate. The 30 finalists receiving the $5,000 scholarships receive their award money upon graduation from high school.

In order to participate in this program, students must be in their last year of high school and have completed their college entrance requirements by October

1 of their senior year. The research project submitted must be the work of a single student (team projects are not eligible). The student's report must not exceed 20 pages along with the research report. The student and his or her teacher or adviser must submit completed entry forms along with the student's official high school transcripts, class rank, and standardized test scores. While every aspect of a student's entry form factors into his or her chances of winning the competition, the research report is given the most weight by the judging panel of prestigious scientists, mathematicians, and engineers. The deadline for submission of all materials is in mid-November of each year.

For more information on this contest or how to obtain forms for participation, contact Science Service, 1719 N Street, N.W., Washington, D.C. 20036. Telephone (202) 785-2255 or visit them online at www.sciserv.org/sts.

Discovery Channel Young Scientist Challenge

The Discovery Channel Young Scientist Challenge (DCYSC) for students in grades 5-8 began in 1999. This competition is administered by Science Service and funded by Discovery Communications, Inc. The top 10 percent of students winning at a state or regional DCYSC affiliated fair are eligible for nomination in the DCYSC. These nominees win various awards and receive an entry booklet for the national competition. Students are required to submit their entries by a June deadline in order to compete to become one of 400 semifinalists. Forty finalists win an all-expense-paid trip to Washington, D.C., to compete for a variety of scholarships, prizes, and internships in the month of October.

For more information on this contest or how to obtain forms for participation, contact Science Service, 1719 N Street, N.W., Washington, D.C. 20036. Telephone (202) 785-2255 or visit them online at www.sciserv.org/dysc.

Siemens Westinghouse Competition

This competition is funded by the Siemens Foundation and is administered by the College Board and Educational Testing Service (the same group that created the SAT). It draws about 1,200 high school contestants annually comprising both individual and team projects. Entries are evaluated purely on scientific merit. Winners from various regional competitions advance to the national level where individual contestants compete for a top prize of a $100,000 scholarship and team projects compete for a top team prize of $100,000 that is split among the team members. In addition to the top scholarship prizes are a number of other significant scholarship prizes for students in second through sixth place as well as smaller cash prizes for regional finalists and winners.

The deadline for submission of application materials is October 1 of every year.

For more information on this contest or how to obtain forms for participation, contact the Siemens Foundation, 170 Wood Ave. South, Iselin, NJ 08830. Telephone (877) 822-5233 or visit them online at www.siemens-foundation.org.

Junior Science and Humanities Symposium

The Junior Science and Humanities Symposium has been sponsored by the U.S. Army since 1958 and was joined in sponsorship by the U.S. Navy and U.S. Air Force in 1995. This competition is open to students in grades 9–12 who have completed a significant research project in science, engineering, or mathematics. Nearly 10,000 students compete annually from the United States and its territories as well as Department of Defense schools in Europe and the Pacific rim. Judging initially occurs at 48 different regional symposiums. To qualify for a regional competition, students must be nominated by their school. Selected students then present their research at the regional level before a panel of judges. The top five winners from each regional competition earn the honor to compete at the National Junior Science and Humanities Symposium for scholarships of various amounts. The top eight national winners also receive an all-expenses-paid trip to the London International Youth Science Forum.

Most regional symposiums have deadlines for school nominations in early December. For more information on this contest or how to obtain forms for participation, contact Junior Science and Humanities Symposium, 24 Warren St., Concord, NH 03301. Telephone (603) 228-4520 or visit them online at www.jshs.org.

GLOSSARY

abstract A brief summary of a science project (approx. 300 words) that explains the project's objective and procedure and provides generalized data and a workable solution to the problem addressed by the project.

backboard A self-supporting bulletin board with a summary outline of a science project. The backboard contains the project title and topic progression, together with flowcharts, photographs, and other significant project descriptions. The backboard is usually organized according to the steps of the scientific method.

biological sciences category A basic category encompassing several life sciences, including behavioral and social sciences, biochemistry, botany, ecology, genetics, medicine and health, microbiology, zoology, animal species studies, disease, etc.

clarity A judging criterion that addresses whether a science project is presented in a concise fashion.

conclusion The solution to a proposed issue and confirmation or rejection of a hypothesis.

control A part of an experiment that provides a guideline for comparing an experimental group.

creative ability A judging criterion that grades ingenuity and originality in an approach to a topic.

data Recorded information that is organized for final analysis and observation.

dependent variable The variable that is being measured.

Discovery Channel Young Scientist Challenge (DCYSC) Since 1999 this science fair, administered by Science Service, has been held for the top science fair projects for students in grades 5–8.

display The complete set-up of a science project. The display includes a backboard, a representation of the subject matter or experimental results, and a research report.

dramatic value A judging criterion that addresses whether the project is presented in a way that attracts attention through the use of graphics and layout.

erroneous hypothesis An incorrect or vague hypothesis that does not support the experimental results.

experiment The part of the project in which the scientist tests to verify a law, explain a cause-and-effect relationship, measure efficiency, or observe an unexplained process.

experimental angle The narrowed experimental option best suited to bringing about a desired or fitting solution to the issue.

flow chart A diagram that describes the results of a process, steps or sequence through the use of various geometric shapes from beginning to end.

frequency distribution   A mathematical summary of a set of data that shows the numerical frequency of each class of items.

histogram   A graph that represents a frequency distribution. The item classes are placed along the horizontal axis and the frequencies along the vertical axis. Rectangles are drawn, with the item class as the base and the frequency as the side.

hypothesis   An assumed or tentative guess as to the possible solution to a problem.

independent variable   The variable that is controlled or manipulated by the experimenter.

Intel International Science and Engineering Fair (Intel ISEF)   Since 1949, this science fair administered by Science Service has been held for the top science fair projects from around the world. It is considered to be the "Super Bowl" of science fairs.

journal   A logbook used to record everything that the student has learned and completed with his or her project. Items to note include articles read, places visited, data results, etc.

line graph   A graph used to summarize information from a table. It has an x (horizontal) axis and a y (vertical) axis, where points are plotted at corresponding regions.

mean   The measurement of the central location of a group of data through the use of a mathematical average. The mean is denoted by the symbol ($\bar{x}$).

percentile   The position of one value from a set of data that expresses the percentage of the other data that lie below this value. The position of a particular percentile can be calculated by dividing the desired percentile by 100 and multiplying by the number of items in the ascending data set.

physical sciences category   A basic category including chemistry, math, earth and space science, engineering, physics, toxic waste, electronics, etc.

pie chart   A graph represented by a circle that is divided into segments. The circle represents the whole amount (100%), and each section represents a percentage of the whole.

primary sources   Those sources of information that consist of surveys, observations, and experiments done directly by the science student.

procedural plan   A uniform and systematic way of testing the subject matter. Procedural planning begins with correlating to determine variables and a uniform control group.

project display   The item(s) from a science project that can fully represent, exemplify, or explain research, experimentation, and conclusions.

project limitation guidelines   Guidelines established by the ISEF that explain how far a student may go in his or her research and experimentation.

purpose/objective   The goal of a project; the theme that requires greater development or understanding.

qualitative analysis   A means of analysis that is based on the findings in an experiment.

quantitative analysis   A means of analysis that is based on measurements in an experiment (always involves numbers).

research   The process by which information about the issue at hand is collected to search for possible clues in the development of the purpose or objective.

research report   An in-depth discussion of an entire science project from start to finish, including a subject history, research experience, method applied, experimental angle used, data, conclusive remarks, glossary, photos, diagrams, etc.

science fair   An exhibition of selectively chosen science projects grouped into corresponding categories and marked for their quality. Science fairs occur on local, state, regional, and international levels. (The fairs discussed in this book refer to those affiliated with the International Science and Engineering Fair.)

science project   A project of a scientific nature that is done by students in grades 6–12 for a local, state, regional, or international science exhibition. The project employs a systematic approach in order to formulate a conclusion to a proposed scientific question. The science project is modeled after the scientific method.

scientific abstracts   Bound volumes of thousands of brief scientific discussions. Scientific abstracts are grouped into two classes: research and experimental. The abstracts discuss experimental reports and review scientific literature.

scientific approach   A judging criterion that addresses how a science project shows evidence of an applied scientific or engineering development through cause-and-effect, verification of laws, applied techniques for efficiency, or presentation of a new concept.

scientific method   An organized process used to form the basis of a science fair project consisting of a problem/purpose, hypothesis, research/procedure, experiment, and conclusion.

scientific review committee (SRC)   A group of science fair officials that enforces various rules and criteria for conducting and completing a science fair project.

secondary sources   Sources of information written by outsiders and obtained through libraries, media, government agencies, or corporations.

skill   A judging criterion that grades a science project on how much scientific and engineering practice was employed. The level of experimentation, preparation, and treatment of the subject matter play an important role.

statistical method   A method used to further describe and summarize data results through the use of specialized numbers, graphs, and charts.

table   An orderly display of data, usually arranged in rows and columns.

tests and surveys   The techniques that endeavor to determine the relationship, if any, that exists between variables.

timeline   A diagram that shows various results or measurements that have been recorded at various stages at specific times.

thoroughness   A judging criterion that addresses the variety and depth of the literature used, experimental investigation, and all the aspects of the project.

variable   Some characteristic of an object, environment, plant, animal, performance, or behavior that can take on two or more values.

INDEX

copper, green tones in light-colored hair caused by, in swimming pools, acid solutions treatment for, 144–147
corrosion, coating prevention, 116–118
currency, cocaine residue on, 108–111

data analysis, 37–43
  flow charts, 42–43
  importance of, 37
  statistical method, 40–42
  tabulation and graphing, 37–40
  time line, 42
dependent variables, 32–33
Discovery Channel Young Scientist Challenge, 8, 219
display, 44–51
  abstract, 48–49
  backboard, 44–46
  report, 46–48
  restrictions on, 49–51

earthworms, 151–153
electromagnetic emissions, cellular phones and safety, 141–143
electronic periodicals, topic selection, 18
engineering, attic ventilation, 103–107
environmental science
  asphalt, peak load evaluation and noise pollution, 90–94
  corrosion of metals, coating prevention of, 116–118
  earthworms, nitrates and phosphates found in fertilized soil, 151–153
  flame retardants for evergreen trees, 137–140
  toilet paper texture and low-flow toilet bowl clogging, 75–77
  wood types, water absorption resistance in natural state with surface coatings, 173–175
erroneous hypothesis, experiments, 35
evergreen trees, flame retardants for, 137–140
expenses, budgeting, 22–23
experiences, topic selection, 16–17
experiments, 28–36
  conducting of, 34–35
  control group, 33–34
  objectives, 29–30

organization, 31–32
procedural plan, 32–33
scientific method, 28
Scientific Review Committee (SRC) approval, 30–31

failed experiments, avoidance of, 34–35
final analysis, experiments, 35
flame retardants, 137–140
flow charts, data analysis, 42–43
forensic scientist, 108
forms
  animal study approvals, 65, 119
  controlled substances, 108
  human studies, 82, 86, 95, 144, 182
  pathogens, 148
  science fair project, 23–24
  Scientific Review Committee (SRC) approval, 30–31
free radicals, antioxidants among teas, 72–74
frequency distribution, 40–41

garlic, vitamin C and, effects on high blood pressure, in humans, 95–98
genetics. See biology
glucose sources, 163–166
graphing, data analysis, 37–40
green tones, in light-colored hair caused by copper in swimming pools, acid solutions treatment for, 144–147

handwriting analysis, 160–162
health and medicine
  body temperature thermometer, accuracy testing, 176–178
  glucose sources for hypoglycemia, 163–166
  high blood pressure, garlic and vitamin C effects, 95–98
heat of reaction, 69–71
high blood pressure, garlic and vitamin C effects on, in humans, 95–98
human studies, approvals for, 82, 86, 95, 144, 182
humidity effects, and temperature effects on sound of church organ, 167–169
hypoglycemia, glucose, 163–166